*The*
*Beer Makes It Better*
*Cook Book*

# *The*
# Beer Makes
# It Better
# Cook Book

Maria Russell and Maxine Stromberg

*Illustrations by Robert Deschamps*

AN ESSANDESS SPECIAL EDITION

*New York*

THE BEER MAKES IT BETTER COOK BOOK
SBN: 671–10503–5
Published by Essandess Special Editions,
a division of Simon & Schuster, Inc.,
630 Fifth Avenue, New York, N.Y. 10020,
and on the same day in Canada
by Simon & Schuster of Canada, Ltd.,
Richmond Hill, Ontario.
Cover photograph by
Irwin Horowitz.
Printed in the U.S.A.

# Contents

# Contents

# Introduction

Although most of us tend to relegate beer and ale to the ordinary everyday category, we have found their rather elegant and unusual flavor a happy experience in cooking. Apart from the classic Belgian stew, Carbonnades de Boeuf, there are numerous fine recipes containing beer for every course that you serve. And there's no need to be concerned about alcoholic content—it evaporates within minutes as beer cooks, leaving a marvelous flavor of grain and hops.

Whether you prefer the delicate flavor of beer from the Scandinavian countries, or the hearty, zestful sip of a Mexican brew, cooking with beer is a delightful custom that goes back for centuries. We all know that beer was a popular beverage among the Egyptians, for historical records found in the valley of the Nile contain recipes for brewing and malting beer. The Romans considered beer a delicate luxury and named it *cerevisia*, or honey-water. Natives in Asia and Africa brew a fairly potent beer with millet and sorghum grains. Americans, on the other hand, seem to prefer a pale pilsner beer. Thus, most of the recipes you'll find in this book call for pilsner beer that can easily be found in cans or bottles in every supermarket.

It's been quite a challenge for us to collect and try every beer recipe we could find. It all began when we followed a recipe for pancakes one day and ran across beer way down on the bottom of the list of ingredients.

We had never seen a cookbook devoted to beer recipes,

7

but the more we experimented, the more we found that beer was actually a very valuable ingredient. And that's how this cookbook was born!

Our next job was to sit down and try all the recipes. We discovered that beer was a different and interesting ingredient, somewhat like a conglomeration of seasonings that could never be put together as a bouquet garni. We had some marvelous success and, naturally, some painful disasters. One teen-age party almost never got off the ground when the Stromberg girls served a cheese fondue that was pure mucilage. (The recipe called for 3 tablespoons of cornstarch—far too much, as we later discovered.) At any rate, we've had a lot of fun trying out all these dishes. We don't claim to be of Cordon Bleu calibre, but we have managed to put our imprint on every page.

As you read through this book, you'll notice that all the dishes are easy to prepare. We're sure you'll agree that even a culinary novice will have an easy time of it if she follows this book. It certainly is adaptable to all tastes and pocketbooks; it can be simple or complicated, economical or extravagant.

We want to thank our many friends for their help and cooperation. They not only pitched in with useful suggestions, but were amiable guinea pigs at tasting time. We are both housewives, and our assorted six children also helped by willingly trying everything at least once. They enjoyed these dishes just as much as our guests at company dinners. Thus, we feel truly confident as we invite you to join us in the world of beer cookery. It's been great fun for both us and our families, and we think you'll enjoy preparing and serving these recipes too.

MARIA RUSSELL AND MAXINE STROMBERG

# Quick Tips on Cooking with Beer

You can use any and every kind of beer for cooking. Just remember that some dark beers are more bitter than the light pilsners, so if you're cooking with dark beer, you may want to reduce your salt seasoning.

Canned or bottled beer may be used. In either case (and this is important), the beer you use for cooking should *not* be refrigerated. If you have already chilled the beer, pour out the desired amount and let it stand until it reaches room temperature. This will make it flat and slightly warm, as it should be.

To add flavor and texture to less expensive cuts of meat (pot roasts, stews, and so on), marinate overnight in beer with enough to cover.

Broiled chicken receives added zest if marinated in beer for a few hours before cooking.

Be adventurous. Try porter, a dark type of beer, somewhat sweeter and less hoppy than regular ale.

Beer has a very low alcoholic content, between 2½ and 5 percent. The alcohol passes off in the heat almost minutes after cooking commences.

Bock beer is a special kind of heavy beer, usually darker and richer than ordinary beer.

Stout is a strong, dark, fully hopped type of porter. It's sweet with a slightly burnt flavor.

Although hop is widely known as a flavoring ingredient in beer, a portion of the hop plant can be used as a vegetable. In Belgium, the hop shoot is used with egg dishes and many other tasty recipes.

Exposing bottled beer to direct sunlight will harm the taste.

*Beauty hint*: Beer is a wonderful hair body-builder. Use it when you set your hair. When your hair dries, there's no beer odor and it really holds the set.

# Hors d'Oeuvres

The simplest meal has a festive touch when you start with an hors d'oeuvre. We think it's vital for any good dinner party. There may be an occasion when you have an extravagant main course and therefore will want a simple beginning, like our Shrimp in Beer; or, you might want to "shoot the works" on a Party Shrimp Pie. Our opening chapter includes appetizers that may be served at the table or as a cocktail accompaniment. However, there are included throughout the book recipes for cheese and vegetable dishes, many of which lend themselves in small portions to appetizers. Fried vegetables in Beer Batter, for example, is an excellent hot hors d'oeuvre.

There are many new taste thrills ahead for the adventurous cook and her guests.

## COCKTAIL PUFFS

1 cup beer
¼ pound butter
1 cup sifted flour

½ teaspoon salt
4 eggs

Bring beer and butter to a boil. When butter melts, add flour and salt all at once. Cook over low heat, mixing steadily until mixture leaves sides of pan. Remove from heat. Beat in eggs, one at a time, until dough is shiny.

Drop mixture onto a buttered baking sheet with a teaspoon, leaving 1 inch between each puff. Bake in a 450° preheated oven for 10 minutes. Reduce heat to 350° and bake 10 minutes longer until brown.

Cool, then split and fill with crabmeat, cheese mixture, liver pâté, or any desired filling.

*Makes 36 puffs.*

## CHUTNEY CHEESE SPREAD

2 3-ounce packages cream
   cheese, softened
1 cup shredded sharp
   natural Cheddar cheese
2 tablespoons beer
½ teaspoon curry powder

¼ teaspoon salt
¼ cup finely chopped
   chutney
1 tablespoon finely snipped
   chives (or green onion
   tops)

Combine cheeses and blend well. Add beer, curry powder, and salt. Mix. Stir in chutney. Chill. Pour into serving dish and top with chives. (If necessary, thin with more beer.)

This is excellent with crackers and fresh fruit as a dessert.

*Makes about 1⅔ cups.*

## CHILI WITH CHEESE DIP

2 *medium onions, chopped*
2 *tablespoons salad oil*
2 *medium tomatoes,*
    *chopped*
1 *clove garlic, chopped*
1 *small can pimientos,*
    *chopped*

2 *small cans peeled peppers,*
    *chopped*
¼ *cup condensed milk*
2 *pounds Velveeta cheese*
¼ *cup beer*

Fry onions in oil but do not brown. Add tomatoes and garlic, then simmer ½ hour. Add pimientos and peppers, then simmer another ½ hour.

Add milk and cheese; when cheese is melted, add beer. Serve with king-size corn chips.

*Makes about 2 cups.*

## ROQUEFORT CHEESE BALL

1 *pound Roquefort cheese*
2 *3-ounce packages cream*
    *cheese*
1 *tablespoon finely minced*
    *onion*

1 *teaspoon Worcestershire*
    *sauce*
5 *drops Tabasco sauce*
2 *tablespoons beer*
1½ *cups chopped walnuts*

Soften Roquefort and cream cheese, then blend together until very smooth. Mix in onion, Worcestershire sauce, Tabasco sauce, and beer. Stir well. Chill for about 1 hour.

Shape into 1 large ball or 2 small ones and roll in chopped nuts. Cover well with foil and refrigerate until serving time.

(This recipe may be made up several days in advance.)

*Serves 12.*

## DILL DIP

1 3-ounce package cream
cheese
1 tablespoon finely chopped
green olives

1 teaspoon grated onion
¼ teaspoon dried dill weed
Dash salt
1–2 tablespoons beer

Soften cream cheese and stir well. Add olives, onion, dill weed, and salt. Stir well and add first tablespoon of beer. If not dipping consistency, add second tablespoon of beer, or a little more.

Serve with celery, carrot sticks, and so forth, as an appetizer.

*Makes about ⅔ cup.*

## CHIPPER BEER CHEESE

This is a marvelous cheese blend that takes days to make but is certainly worth the effort. It can be made well in advance and keeps in the refrigerator for weeks; you'll find it a gem for spur-of-the-moment snacks!

3 pounds Cheddar cheese
3 medium onions
½ cup Worcestershire sauce

¼ cup Tabasco sauce
¾ cup stale beer

Break cheese into chunks and spread out on cookie tray; let dry out for 6 hours. Put cheese through medium blade of food chopper. Put onions through fine blade of chopper. Blend onion and cheese. Chill overnight in refrigerator, uncovered.

Combine Worcestershire sauce and Tabasco sauce with cheese mixture. Blend well and chill 4 hours. Blend again and chill overnight.

Blend cheese thoroughly with ½ cup stale beer and chill for 3 hours.

Blend ¼ cup beer into mixture and bring to spreading consistency. Chill. Let stand 2 to 3 days in refrigerator, adding a little more beer from time to time if cheese becomes dry.

Serve with crackers.

*Makes about 3 cups.*

## CHEESE DIP DUO

| | |
|---|---|
| 2 *pounds Cheddar cheese,* *shredded* | 1 *teaspoon Worcestershire* *sauce* |
| 4 *ounces Roquefort cheese* | 1 *tablespoon chopped chives* |
| 1 *teaspoon dry mustard* | *(or grated onion)* |
| ¼ *teaspoon Tabasco sauce* | 1 *cup beer* |

Be sure cheese is softened by letting it stand at room temperature 30 minutes. Place all ingredients except beer in a mixing bowl and, using electric mixer, blend slowly, gradually adding beer until smooth and creamy. Chill several hours in covered container.

Serve with crackers or thinly sliced rye bread.

*Makes about 2 cups.*

## AUSTRIAN CHEDDAR TRIANGLES

| | |
|---|---|
| 6 *slices firm white bread* | 2 *teaspoons catsup* |
| ¾ *cup beer* | 2 *teaspoons flour* |
| 3 *eggs* | 1 *teaspoon paprika* |
| 5 *ounces Cheddar cheese,* *grated* | 4 *tablespoons butter* |

Soak bread on both sides in beer. Beat eggs and add cheese, catsup, flour, and paprika. Mix well.

Melt butter in large skillet. Spread half the cheese mixture on one side only of beer-soaked bread. Place bread, cheese side down, in skillet, and fry until golden.

While bread is frying, spread remaining mixture on top of each slice. Then turn slices and fry on second side. Cut each slice into fours and serve at once.

*Serves 6.*

## STUFFED BREAD CANAPES

| | |
|---|---|
| 1 *large loaf French or Italian* | ¼ *cup beer* |
| *bread* | 1 *tablespoon dry mustard* |
| ½ *pound liverwurst* | ¼ *cup chopped watercress* |
| 2 *8-ounce packages cream* | ¼ *cup chopped onion* |
| *cheese, softened* | ¼ *cup chopped radishes* |

Preheat oven to 350°. Cut loaf of bread crosswise into three large pieces. Cut off ends and discard. Scoop out center part of bread, leaving ¼-inch-thick shell crust. Crumble cut-out bread into small pieces and toast on a cookie sheet about 15 minutes until bread is lightly browned.

Cut liverwurst into small cubes. Stir cream cheese until soft. Mix beer and mustard into cream cheese. Add watercress, onion, and radishes, and mix well. Lightly mix in liverwurst.

When browned bread crumbs are cool, stir into cheese mixture. Pack stuffing into bread shells and wrap up each piece of bread in aluminum foil. Refrigerate 4 hours. Unwrap, slice thin, and serve.

*Serves 8.*

## BASIC CHEESE SPREAD

Here is a good basic cheese spread that is sure to perk up appetites. It can be served on crackers, thinly sliced rye bread, or pumpernickel. Be highly individual and add either a small can of chopped anchovies, chopped pimiento, coarsely chopped olives, gherkins, or capers. A teaspoon of caraway seeds will change the flavor too. If you want a dip instead of a spread, use more beer to thin your mixture.

1 *cup sweet butter*

2 *3-ounce packages cream cheese with chives*

¼ *pound Roquefort or blue cheese*

¼ *cup flat beer*

½ *teaspoon Tabasco sauce*

½ *teaspoon dry mustard*

Soften butter and cheese to room temperature and blend well in a small bowl. Add remaining ingredients, with perhaps one of the additions suggested above. Mix well.

*Makes about 2 cups.*

## ALMOND AND CHEESE DIP

1 *3-ounce package cream cheese*

½ *cup crumbled blue cheese*

3 *tablespoons beer*

1 *teaspoon Worcestershire sauce*

½ *clove garlic, crushed*

½ *cup chopped black olives*

½ *cup blanched and chopped almonds*

Soften cream cheese to room temperature and blend with blue cheese. Add remaining ingredients. If too thick for spreading, add 2 tablespoons more beer.

Serve with assorted crackers.

*Makes about 1 cup.*

## HAM MOUSSE

| | |
|---|---|
| 1 *envelope unflavored gelatin* | 2 *4½ -ounce cans deviled ham* |
| ⅔ *cup beer* | 1 *teaspoon mustard* |
| 4 *ounces blue cheese, crumbled* | 1 *tablespoon minced onion* |
| 1 *cup cottage cheese* | ½ *teaspoon Tabasco sauce* |
| | ½ *cup heavy cream* |

Dissolve gelatin in beer over low heat in saucepan. Cool. Line 4-cup mold with tin foil.

Combine cheeses, ham, mustard, onion, and Tabasco sauce. Beat with an electric mixer until smooth. Stir in beer mixture.

Whip cream and gently fold into cheese mixture. Turn into mold and chill until firm.

Garnish with parsley or sliced olives and serve with assorted crackers and breads.

*Serves 18 to 20.*

## STUFFED SHRIMP APPETIZERS

| | |
|---|---|
| 3 *pounds large shrimp, shelled and deveined* | ½ *cup (3 ounces) blue cheese* |
| 1 *3-ounce package cream cheese* | ⅓ *cup beer* |
| | ¼ *cup minced parsley* |

Cook shrimp in boiling, salted water 5 to 10 minutes. Drain, cool, and chill.

Blend cheeses together and gradually stir in beer. Slit shrimp partway along vein side. Stuff with cheese mixture.

Roll cheese side in parsley.

*Serves 12.*

## PARTY SHRIMP PIE

Here is a good recipe for a first course that might be served along with cocktails or ice-cold beer.

5 *pounds raw shrimp,*
   *shelled and deveined*
1 *cup stale beer*
1 *bay leaf*
1 *teaspoon dried thyme*
1 *tablespoon plus* ½
   *teaspoon salt*
1 *onion, sliced*
½ *cup butter*

½ *cup flour*
1 *quart milk*
1 *cup light cream*
¼ *teaspoon black pepper*
⅛ *teaspoon curry powder*
1 *cup pitted ripe olives*
½ *cup blanched almonds*
*Pastry for one large pie shell*

Cook shrimp in a large pot with beer, bay leaf, thyme, 1 tablespoon salt, onion, and enough boiling water to cover. Simmer 5 minutes and cool shrimp in liquid.

Melt butter in saucepan and add flour, stirring constantly. Add 2 cups of strained shrimp liquid, plus milk, cream, ½ teaspoon salt, pepper, and curry powder. Cook until thickened and then add cooked shrimp, olives, and almonds.

Place shrimp mixture in a large baking pan (approximately 10″ x 14″ x 3″) and cover with rolled-out pastry dough. Bake at 375° until crust is browned.

*Serves 12 to 16.*

## SHRIMP IN BEER #1

2 *pounds raw shrimp*
1 *12-ounce can beer*
2 *dried red peppers*

2 *bay leaves*
¼ *teaspoon thyme*

Place shrimp in a saucepan with beer to cover and bring

to boil. Add peppers and herbs. Simmer 5 minutes, covered. Do not drain. Cool shrimp in liquid; discard liquid. Shell, devein, and chill.

Serve with your favorite sauce, but the taste is superb without any sauce.

*Serves 8.*

## SHRIMP IN BEER #2

3 *pounds raw shrimp*          *Fresh celery leaves*
1 *12-ounce can beer*          1 *bay leaf*
3 *sprigs fresh dill*          12 *peppercorns*

Wash shrimp and place in saucepan with beer to cover. Bring to a boil. Add dill, celery leaves, bay leaf, and peppercorns. Simmer 3 minutes.

Let shrimp cool in broth and serve in individual soup plates with some of the liquid. Or, drain, shell, devein, and serve with your favorite sauce.

*Serves 12.*

## HOT SHRIMP HORS D'OEUVRES

2 *pounds raw shrimp,*          2 *tablespoons flour*
   *shelled and deveined*          1 *cup beer*
3 *tablespoons chopped onion*          3 *tablespoons lemon juice*
4 *tablespoons butter*          1 *bay leaf*
1½ *teaspoons salt*          2 *teaspoons parsley*
¼ *teaspoon Tabasco sauce*

Dry shrimp and sauté with onion in butter for 2 minutes, or until pink. Add salt, Tabasco sauce, and flour. Slowly add beer and lemon juice, stirring constantly. Bring to boil. Add bay leaf and cook over low heat 5 minutes. Discard bay leaf. Remove to serving dish, sprinkle with parsley, and serve on toothpicks.

*Serves 8.*

## DEVILED CLAMS

24 *clams on the half shell*
6 *tablespoons butter*
3 *tablespoons minced onion*
1 *clove garlic, minced*
1 *tablespoon minced parsley*

¼ *cup beer*
4 *slices crisp bacon,*
  *crumbled*
4 *tablespoons bread crumbs*

Chop the clams coarsely. Cream together the butter, onion, garlic, and parsley. Blend in beer, then add bacon and clams.

Fill clam shells with mixture and sprinkle with bread crumbs. Place on cookie sheet and bake at 375° 10 minutes, or until thoroughly heated through.

*Serves 4 to 6.*

## COCKTAIL CLAM FRITTERS

1½ *cups flour*
½ *teaspoon salt*
8 *tablespoons butter*
3 *eggs, separated*
¾ *cup beer*
2 *cups canned minced clams*

1 *tablespoon finely chopped*
  *parsley*
1 *tablespoon finely chopped*
  *chives*
*Lemon wedges*
*Parsley sprigs*

Mix flour and salt in large bowl. Melt 4 tablespoons butter and add to flour. Lightly beat egg yolks and mix with flour.

Slowly add beer and blend. Allow to stand in warm place 1 hour.

Drain clams well and add to batter with parsley and chives. Beat egg whites until stiff, and fold in.

Melt 4 tablespoons butter in pan and drop in batter by spoonfuls. Brown fritters lightly on all sides, and drain on paper towels.

Serve hot, garnished with lemon wedges and parsley sprigs.

*Makes about 36 fritters.*

## SAUSAGES WITH MUSTARD SAUCE DIP

This Mustard Sauce Dip is a hearty, full-flavored beginning for any meal. Use it with Vienna sausages, browned Italian sausages, or ready-to-serve cocktail franks. It should be served hot from the pan and you might want to keep it very warm by placing your sauce in a chafing dish. If you do and it tends to thicken, just thin with beer.

| | |
|---|---|
| ¼ *cup dry mustard* | 1 *teaspoon caraway seeds* |
| 4 *teaspoons cornstarch* | 1 *12-ounce can beer* |
| 1 *tablespoon sugar* | 2 *tablespoons vinegar* |

Blend all ingredients in a saucepan over medium heat until thick, stirring constantly. Remove to warm serving dish.

Serve with canned Vienna sausage or browned sausages, on toothpicks.

*Note:* Cocktail franks or Vienna sausages may be preheated in beer (enough to cover), for the flavor of beer is delicate and unique.

*Makes 1½ cups.*

## SAUSAGES IN PIQUANT SAUCE

1 12-ounce can beer
½ medium onion, minced
¼ teaspoon freshly ground
    pepper
1½ tablespoons brown
    sugar

2 pounds Polish sausage,
    cut in ½-inch pieces
1 tablespoon cornstarch
2 tablespoons fresh minced
    parsley

Set aside 2 tablespoons of beer, then combine rest of beer, onion, pepper, and brown sugar in a saucepan. Simmer sausage in beer mixture 15 minutes.

Mix cornstarch in reserved beer and add to simmering sausages. Stir until thickened.

Sprinkle with minced parsley and serve hot in a chafing dish with cocktail forks or toothpicks.

*Serves 12.*

## PIQUANT COCKTAIL FRANKS

1 14-ounce bottle catsup
4 tablespoons margarine
Dash Worcestershire sauce

6 ounces beer
2 pounds small cocktail
    frankfurters

In a small saucepan, combine all ingredients except frankfurters; stir and simmer over low heat 1 hour. Add frankfurters and heat thoroughly.

We suggest that this be transferred to a chafing dish or heatproof casserole where it may be kept warm for many hours.

*Serves 12 to 16.*

25

## MARINATED MUSHROOMS

Surprisingly easy to prepare, this dish can be made well in advance and served on crackers, or just pierced with toothpicks.

1 *pound raw small white mushrooms, stems removed*
⅔ *cup olive or salad oil*
⅓ *cup beer*
2 *tablespoons lemon juice*
2 *tablespoons instant minced onion*

1 *tablespoon chopped parsley*
¼ *teaspoon oregano, crushed*
½ *teaspoon salt*
⅛ *teaspoon pepper*
1 *large clove garlic, minced*

Place mushrooms in a large, clean jar. Combine remaining ingredients and pour over mushrooms. Cover tightly. Shake jar to make sure all mushrooms are coated with marinade and allow to stand at room temperature for about 3 hours. Store in refrigerator. Mushrooms will keep about 1 week.

*Serves 4 to 6.*

## PARTY BEER TOMATOES

1 *pint cherry tomatoes*
1 *cup beer*

¼ *cup coarse salt*

Wash tomatoes, leaving stems intact. Dip tomatoes in beer and then in salt. Arrange carefully on a serving dish.

*Makes 1 pint.*

# Soups

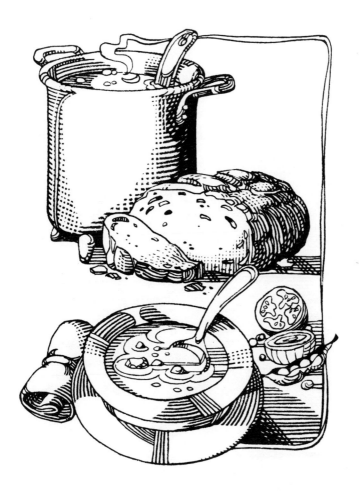

Soup can add a bright beginning to any meal; but many soups, because they are so full-bodied and nutritional, can serve as a main course. You will find some of these hearty recipes in this chapter. Serve them with crusty French bread, fruit or salad, and dessert.

Where stock or broth is required, the canned variety, or granules, or cubes, are an excellent substitute for homemade. There are times, however, when you might find it convenient to use the wings, giblets, and backs of chicken plus seasonings to brew a small pot of stock. Try saving giblets, necks, and extra chicken parts in the freezer. When you have a sizable quantity, cook a large pot of stock that can be jarred and set aside for soups, gravies, or sauces. A well-seasoned stock is the backbone of a great soup.

## BELGIAN BEER SOUP

Here is a speedy recipe that is a hearty soup with a rather interesting flavor. For a slight change of taste substitute a 12-ounce bottle of malt liquor for the beer.

| | |
|---|---|
| 3 *carrots, finely diced* | 2 *cans split pea soup with* |
| 2 *stalks celery, finely diced* | *ham* |
| 1 *medium onion, chopped* | 1 *12-ounce can beer* |
| ½ *stick butter* | 1 *cup beef broth* |

Sauté carrots, celery, and onion in butter until mixture is golden brown and carrots are tender. Meanwhile, combine soup, beer, and beef broth, and simmer over low heat 10 minutes. Add vegetables and cook 5 more minutes.

*Serves 6.*

## LEMON CREAM SOUP

This dish is "iffy". . . . If you want a sweet and sour taste, go light on sugar. However, if you prefer a creamy, not too pungent taste, add a little more sugar. This one is up to you! Be creative—try it both ways.

| | |
|---|---|
| 1 *pint dark lager beer* | 1 *pint milk* |
| *Juice of ½ lemon* | *Sugar to taste (start with 1* |
| *Pinch cinnamon* | *teaspoon)* |
| 2 *egg yolks* | *Salt* |

Heat beer in saucepan with lemon juice and pinch of cinnamon.

Beat egg yolks. Heat milk separately. Slowly blend egg yolks into milk. Add to beer mixture. Season with sugar and salt to taste.

*Serves 4.*

## BEER CHEESE SOUP

¼ *cup celery*

¼ *cup diced carrots*

¼ *cup diced green peppers*

¼ *cup diced onions*

¼ *cup melted butter*

6 *tablespoons flour*

6 *cups chicken broth*

¼ *teaspoon black pepper*

1 *14-ounce bottle sharp cheese spread*

¼ *cup chopped pimiento*

1 *12-ounce can beer*

½ *teaspoon salt*

Cook celery, carrots, green peppers, and onions in butter until tender, not brown. Stir in flour. Slowly stir in broth and pepper. Stir until thickened. Cook over low heat 20 minutes.

Add cheese and stir until melted. Add pimiento. Just before serving, add beer and heat. Season with salt.

*Serves 6 to 8.*

## CINNAMON-BEER SOUP

1 *quart beer*

6 *egg yolks, beaten*

½ *cup light cream*

1 *cup sugar*

1 *teaspoon cinnamon*

Warm beer in top of double boiler (but don't let it get hot). Slowly add beaten egg yolks, stirring constantly. Add cream and sugar; continue stirring. As soup thickens, add cinnamon. Serve at once.

*Serves 4.*

## BACK BAY BEER SOUP

Company coming on the spur of the moment? Here's an elegant quick recipe that's great on a cold wintry night.

| | |
|---|---|
| 1 *can condensed tomato* | 1 *12-ounce can beer* |
|   *soup* | 6 *ounces light cream* |
| 1 *can condensed pea soup* | ½ *cup crabmeat* |

Mix soups together with beer and cream and heat thoroughly, but do not boil. Just before serving, add crabmeat and stir in well.

*Serves 4.*

## BEER SOUP A LA RUSSE

| | |
|---|---|
| 2½ *cups sour cream* | ½ *teaspoon chopped* |
| 2 *tablespoons flour* |   *scallions* |
| ½ *teaspoon salt* | 2 *cups beer* |

In a saucepan blend all ingredients, except beer, until smooth. Gradually stir in beer. Cook, stirring constantly, until hot. Do not boil!

Serve with dark bread or crackers.

*Serves 4.*

## GERMAN LENTIL SOUP

| | |
|---|---|
| 2 *cups lentils* | 1 *bay leaf* |
| 1½ *quarts water* | 2 *tablespoons butter* |
| 1 *pint beer* | 2 *tablespoons flour* |
| ½ *pound salt pork or* | 1 *tablespoon salt* |
|   *hambone* | ¼ *teaspoon freshly ground* |
| 1 *cup chopped celery* |   *pepper* |
| 1 *cup chopped onion* | ½ *cup chopped parsley* |
| ½ *teaspoon dried thyme* | |

Wash lentils and drain. Place in large kettle with water, beer, and salt pork. Cover and simmer 3 hours.

Add celery, onion, thyme, and bay leaf. Cover and simmer 30 minutes longer. Remove bay leaf and salt pork. Put soup through sieve or purée in a blender.

Melt butter in a saucepan; blend in flour, and add a little of the soup. Mix well. Stir mixture back into rest of soup and simmer 10 minutes. Add salt and pepper. Top each portion with parsley and serve.

*Serves 8 to 10.*

## VIENNESE BEER SOUP

| | |
|---|---|
| 3 *cups beer* | 3 *egg yolks* |
| ¾ *cup sugar* | 3 *cups milk* |

Simmer beer 4 minutes, then remove from heat. Beat sugar and egg yolks into the milk. Add to beer. Return soup to heat, but do not let it come to a boil. While heating, beat with an egg beater until soup is smooth and foaming. Serve at once.

*Serves 6.*

## SWEDISH BEER SOUP

This is a strangely pungent sweet soup which is served in Sweden as a dessert. According to old-country custom, it is frequently the Good Friday dessert. It's one of those dishes you'll either like very much or not at all. The woody covering of cardamon seeds has a peculiarly pleasing aroma in this combination.

| | |
|---|---|
| 2 *quarts milk* | ¼ *teaspoon ginger* |
| ½ *cup flour* | 10 *or* 12 *whole cardamon* |
| 1 *12-ounce can beer or ale* | *seeds* |
| ½ *cup molasses* | |

Rinse a soup kettle in cold water to prevent milk from scorching. Pour 6 cups of milk into kettle and bring to a boil, stirring frequently. Stir remaining amount of milk into flour until a smooth, thin paste. Add paste to boiling milk, stirring briskly to prevent lumps. Lower heat and let soup simmer 10 minutes.

In a separate pan, bring beer, molasses, and seasonings to a boil. Pour beer mixture into milk kettle, beating vigorously with an egg beater the entire time.

Taste for additional sweetness. Serve frothing in soup plates with ginger snaps as a garnish.

*Serves 8.*

## KISS OF THE HOPS SOUP

This unusual soup just hits the spot after a brisk bout of raking leaves, shoveling snow, or doing any invigorating exercise.

| | |
|---|---|
| 8 *slices dark rye or pumpernickel bread* | 2 *teaspoons sugar* |
| 2 *cups water* | 2 *egg yolks* |
| 2 *envelopes instant beef broth* | 1 *12-ounce can beer* |
| | *Lemon peel* |

Break up bread slices and place in a 3-quart pan. Add water and heat slowly, using a spoon to break the bread into tiny pieces. Add instant broth and sugar. Lightly beat egg yolks in a bowl and add beer. Pour a small amount of the bread mixture into the beer mixture; stir, then return all to pan. Stir over low heat until boiling point is reached.

Pour soup into mugs or bowls, and float crisp bread chunks topped with twists of lemon peel. *Skoal!*

*Serves 4.*

# Beef

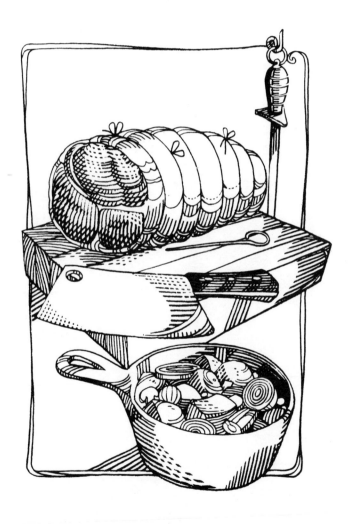

The most nutritious of all meats and the one best adapted to delicate constitutions is beef. Americans are beef-loving people, many of whom are devotees of the barbecued variety. For this reason, we've included recipes for the steak and hot-dog lovers—but a large portion of this chapter concentrates on the more exotic Belgian *carbonnades.* There are many variations of this well-known Flemish dish and each has its own special style and flavor. Each one provides a unique taste experience when served with boiled parsley potatoes or buttered noodles, a green salad, and, for those who are so inclined, lots of ice-cold beer.

Many of our beef dishes require the less expensive cuts of beef. For the inevitable chopped-beef dinner that nearly everyone includes in the weekly menu, we discovered some recipes that are pure joy! What a delight to turn from the tired meat loaf and hamburger dinners to Nordic Meatballs or Curried Beef Stroganoff Balls.

You can honestly add some very exciting notes to your menus while you maintain the restrictions of your budget. Try Beef au Beer, one of our favorite combinations. This should convince the most skeptical.

## CARBONNADES DE BOEUF

3 *pounds chuck cut into*
*2-inch cubes*
½ *cup flour*
1 *teaspoon salt*
½ *teaspoon pepper*
8 *tablespoons butter*
2 *cups beer*

2 *tablespoons red wine*
*vinegar*
¼ *cup chopped parsley*
1 *teaspoon thyme*
1 *bay leaf, crumbled*
4–6 *large onions, sliced*
1 *teaspoon sugar*

Dredge meat in flour seasoned with salt and pepper; brown in 3 tablespoons butter. Add beer, vinegar, parsley, thyme, and bay leaf, and simmer covered 1 to 1½ hours. Liquid should cover meat, so add more beer if necessary.

In large skillet, melt rest of butter, add onions and sugar, and cook over low heat until onions are glazed and clear (15 to 20 minutes). Add to meat and simmer covered 1 hour, or until gravy is thickened. If meat begins to stick to bottom, do not add more liquid at this point; keep stirring frequently and cook a shorter period of time, enough to blend onion flavor into meat.

*Serves 6 to 8.*

## CARBONNADE A LA FLAMANDE #1

2½ *pounds beef rump or*
*chuck*
3 *tablespoons butter or oil*
3 *large onions, sliced*
1 *tablespoon brown sugar*
2 *tablespoons vinegar*
1 *clove garlic, chopped*

½ *teaspoon thyme*
1 *bay leaf*
2 *cups beer*
1–2 *tablespoons Dijon*
*mustard*
1 *slice stale bread*

Cut beef into 10 to 14 slices and flatten them. Brown meat

in butter in a skillet and place in 2½-quart heavy casserole. Lightly brown onions in fat remaining in skillet, sprinkle with brown sugar, and shake skillet over medium heat until sugar melts. Add vinegar.

Add contents of skillet to casserole. Place garlic, thyme, and bay leaf over meat. Cover meat completely with beer. Spread mustard thickly on slice of bread and place on top of beef.

Cover casserole, bring to boil, then reduce heat and simmer gently 2 hours. The beer should then be reduced by half. If necessary, remove cover for last 15 minutes. The bread dissolves and binds the sauce.

*Serves 6.*

## CARBONNADE A LA FLAMANDE #2

3 *pounds beef rump or chuck*
2–3 *tablespoons fresh pork fat or cooking oil*
6 *cups sliced onions*
*Salt and pepper*
4 *cloves garlic, mashed*
1 *cup beef stock or bouillon*
2–3 *cups light beer (pilsner preferred)*

2 *tablespoons light brown sugar*
1 *bouquet garni (6 parsley sprigs, 1 bay leaf, ½ teaspoon thyme tied in cheesecloth)*
1½ *tablespoons cornstarch blended with*
2 *tablespoons wine vinegar*

Slice beef into pieces 2 x 4 inches and ½ inch thick. Heat fat or oil in a heavy skillet or electric frying pan. Brown slices quickly and set them aside. Lower heat and stir onions into fat remaining in skillet, adding more fat if needed; brown lightly, remove from heat, and stir in salt, pepper, and garlic.

Combine beef and onions in a 3-quart heatproof casserole. Heat stock in skillet, scraping all remaining food particles. Pour over meat and add beer. Stir in brown sugar and bury bouquet garni in casserole. Bring casserole to boil on top of stove, then cover and place in 325° oven for approximately 2½ hours.

Remove bouquet garni, drain liquid into a saucepan, and skim off fat. Briskly stir in starch and vinegar mixture and simmer a few minutes. Adjust seasonings if necessary. Spoon sauce over meat and serve.

*Serves 6 to 8.*

## BACHELOR'S STEAK

| | |
|---|---|
| 1 *thick porterhouse steak* | 1 *pound mushrooms (fresh* |
| *Olive oil* | *or canned)* |
| *Vinegar* | 4 *tablespoons butter* |
| *Salt and pepper* | 2 *tablespoons flour* |
| | 2 *cups beer* |

Rub steak with oil and vinegar, season on both sides with salt and pepper, and let stand in refrigerator. For a 2-inch steak, broil 6 to 12 minutes on each side in a preheated broiler.

A few minutes before steak is done, sauté sliced mushrooms in butter, season with salt and pepper, add flour, steak juice from broiler pan, and beer. Stir well while cooking. Let come to a boil, pour over steak, and serve.

*Serves 4.*

## BROILED STEAK WITH TEXAS STEAK SAUCE

⅔ cup catsup
½ cup beer
2–3 teaspoons
  Worcestershire sauce
2 drops liquid smoke
3 tablespoons butter

Tabasco sauce to taste
2 pounds sirloin steak,
  1-inch thick
1 clove garlic
Salt and pepper

Combine catsup, beer, Worcestershire sauce, liquid smoke, and 1 tablespoon butter. Simmer until thickened (about 30 minutes). Add Tabasco sauce just before serving.

Rub steak with garlic. While sauce is cooking, grill or broil steak about 4 to 6 inches from heat, to desired doneness. Season with salt and pepper and spread rest of butter on each side. Serve with sauce.

*Serves 2 to 3.*

## OVEN-BREWED BEEF

2–3 slices bacon
2 medium onions
3½–4-pound rump roast
1 cup beer
1 cup water
½ cup vinegar

1 tablespoon brown sugar
½ teaspoon salt
6 peppercorns
3 cloves
2 bay leaves

Line bottom of oven-proof casserole with bacon. Slice onions and place on top of bacon. Add meat and cover with mixture consisting of remaining ingredients.

Preheat oven to 300° and bake 3 hours.

*Serves 6 to 8.*

## FLEMING BEEF STEW

2½ pounds beef chuck cut
    into 1½-inch cubes
½ cup seasoned flour
3 tablespoons melted
    shortening
4 medium onions, sliced
½ cup butter

3 tablespoons flour
1 12-ounce can dark beer
2 cloves garlic
1 bay leaf
3 sprigs parsley
½ teaspoon thyme

Dredge beef cubes in seasoned flour and brown in melted shortening in a large skillet. Remove and set aside. Cook onions in skillet in ½ cup butter. Remove onions. Add 3 tablespoons flour to butter remaining in skillet and cook, stirring constantly, until blended. Add beer and bring to boil until thickened.

Return meat and onions to skillet and add remaining ingredients. Cover and cook over low heat 2½ hours, or until beef is tender.

*Serves 6.*

## BEEF AU BEER

12 small onions (fresh or
    canned)
1 pound mushrooms
6 tablespoons butter or
    margarine
2 pounds lean beef
1½ tablespoons flour
1 tablespoon brown sugar

2 teaspoons prepared
    mustard
4 peppercorns
2 bay leaves
½ teaspoon salt
2¼ cups beer
Chopped parsley

In a heavy pot or skillet, sauté onions and mushrooms in butter. Remove and set aside. Add beef and cook until brown. Sprinkle with flour, brown sugar, and mustard. Add remaining ingredients. Cover and chill until ready to bake.

Preheat oven to 275°. Bake meat for 1 hour. Add onions and mushrooms, and bake 30 minutes more, or until beef is tender (you may also let it simmer on top of the stove for the same length of time). Adjust seasonings if necessary. Sprinkle with chopped parsley.

*Serves 4 to 6.*

## BEEF BRISKET

| | |
|---|---|
| 3½–4 *pounds beef brisket* | ¾ *cup catsup* |
| 1 *12-ounce can beer* | 1 *large onion* |

Place brisket in shallow baking dish and bake at 325° ½ hour. Drain fat. Pour beer over brisket, cover top with catsup, and slice an onion over it. Cover baking dish tightly and lower oven to 250°. Bake 4 hours.

(You can use double strength tin foil to cover baking dish, but do keep foil tightly closed.)

*Serves 6 to 8.*

## BEEF AND VEGETABLES

| | |
|---|---|
| ⅓ *cup flour* | 1 *tablespoon Worcestershire* |
| 2 *teaspoons salt* | *sauce* |
| ¼ *teaspoon pepper* | 6 *carrots, pared and cut in* |
| ½ *teaspoon garlic salt* | *large pieces* |
| 2 *pounds beef, cubed* | 4 *medium onions, quartered* |
| ¼ *cup shortening* | ¾ *cup ale* |
| 1 *1-pound can tomatoes* | 1 *package frozen peas* |

Mix flour with seasonings and coat meat. Brown in shortening and pour off remaining fat. Add liquid from canned tomatoes and Worcestershire sauce. Cover and simmer 1 hour.

Add carrots and onions and simmer 1 hour longer.

Pour in ale and add tomatoes and peas. Cook until meat is tender, or another ½ hour.

*Serves 6.*

## POT ROAST

3–5 *pound round roast*           3 *cups beer*
   (*bottom or top*)              1 *cup vinegar*
3 *cloves garlic*                 ¼ *cup cooking oil or fat*

Make long slits on either side of roast and insert garlic pieces. Put roast in a bowl and cover with marinade of 1 cup beer and 1 cup vinegar. Marinate overnight in refrigerator.

Heat fat or cooking oil in a large Dutch oven and brown roast very quickly. Add 2 cups beer and simmer on top of stove 3 hours. If more liquid is needed, add a little more beer. Strain juices and thicken for gravy, if desired.

Vegetables of your choice may be added for final 40 minutes.

*Serves 4 to 8.*

## BEER ROAST

6 *pounds top round roast*        4 *tablespoons salad oil*
*Salt, pepper, and garlic salt*   1 *12-ounce can beer*
   *to taste*                     1½ *tablespoons*
⅓ *cup flour*                        *Worcestershire sauce*

Season roast with salt, pepper, and garlic salt; add flour. Heat oil in heavy Dutch oven; brown meat on all sides. Roast uncovered at 400° 1 hour. Turn roast and pour beer and Worcestershire sauce over it. Return to oven uncovered 45 minutes more. Turn roast again, cover, and cook 1 hour longer. Add more beer if needed to keep from burning.
*Serves 8 to 10.*

## BEEF RECHAUFFE

In these days of high food prices, it's an art to give leftover meats a new hat to wear. The literal translation of *réchauffé* is "warmed up," but with the addition of some convenience foods, you'll soon have a quick family or company dish.

1 *envelope dehydrated Swiss-type beef soup mix*
1½ *cups water*
1 *12-ounce can beer*
1 *16-ounce jar small white onions, drained*
1 *small package frozen peas and carrots*
1 *small can mushroom stems and pieces, drained*
1 *teaspoon white horseradish*
¼ *teaspoon powdered thyme*
12 *slices roast beef*

Place soup mix, water, and beer in a pan or electric skillet. Bring mixture to boil, stirring occasionally. Reduce heat and simmer gently 10 minutes. Add onions, peas and carrots, mushrooms, horseradish, and thyme. Cook 10 minutes. While sauce is cooking, roll up slices of beef; tie the slices with string, or secure them with toothpicks. Gently place beef rolls in sauce and heat thoroughly.
Serve with small boiled potatoes or noodles.
*Serves 6 generous portions.*

## CHILI RAGOUT

3 *pounds beef brisket*
1 *teaspoon salt*
½ *teaspoon pepper*
½ *cup chili sauce*
2 *onions, sliced*

2 *stalks celery*
¼ *cup water*
1 *16-ounce can beer*
¼ *cup chopped fresh*
   *parsley*

Place brisket in a casserole; season with salt and pepper. Cover with chili sauce, onion, and celery. Add water and roast uncovered at 350° until brown.

Pour beer over brisket. Cover and continue baking about 3 hours. Remove meat, strain gravy, and add parsley. Slice meat very thin and reheat in gravy.

*Serves 4 to 6.*

## OLD-FASHIONED SWISS STEAK

3 *pounds round steak,*
   *1-inch thick*
¾ *cup flour*
2 *teaspoons salt*
½ *teaspoon pepper*
¼ *teaspoon garlic powder*
3 *tablespoons butter*

1 *bay leaf*
1 *clove*
1 *12-ounce can beer*
2 *tablespoons tomato paste*
6 *potatoes, pared and halved*
12 *small white onions*

Cut steak into six serving pieces. Season flour with salt, pepper, and garlic powder, and pound into steak with Swiss steak mallet.

Melt butter in a Dutch oven or large stew pot, and brown meat on both sides quickly. Add bay leaf, clove, beer, and tomato paste; stir, and cover. Simmer 1 hour. Add potatoes and onions and cook covered 25 minutes.

*Serves 6.*

# Beef

## BEER BLENDER STEW

1 2-pound round steak,
  1 inch thick
1½ 12-ounce cans beer
3 tablespoons bacon grease
1 teaspoon whole
  peppercorns
1 teaspoon cumin seeds

3 cloves garlic
1 onion, diced
1 green pepper, diced
2 tablespoons flour
1 1-pound can tomatoes
1 teaspoon salt

Cube round steak and marinate 1 hour in 1 can of beer. Drain. Melt bacon grease and brown meat well.

Blend peppercorns, cumin seeds, and garlic in blender until a paste is formed. Set aside. To the meat, add onion, green pepper, flour, tomatoes, salt, and blended seasonings. Add additional ½ can of beer and enough water to almost cover meat. Simmer 45 minutes. If necessary, add a bit more beer as needed so there will be gravy.

Serves 6.

## BEEF MORGAN #1

2 pounds round steak, cut
  into 2-inch cubes
Flour
1 teaspoon salt
6 tablespoons cooking oil
1 cup thinly sliced onion

1 10¾-ounce can condensed
  tomato soup
1 12-ounce can beer
Spice bag of bay leaf, 5
  cloves, pinch thyme

Dredge meat in flour and salt mixture and brown in cooking oil. Add onion, tomato soup, beer, and spice bag, and simmer, covered, 2 hours.

Remove spice bag and serve with spinach noodles.

Serves 4 to 5.

## BEEF MORGAN #2

4–5 *pound boneless pot*     *Vegetable oil to cover*
   *roast*     *bottom of pot*
2 *tablespoons prepared*     1 *large onion, sliced*
   *mustard*     1 *12-ounce can beer*
*Salt and pepper to taste*     1 *cup sour cream*

Cover meat with mustard, salt, and pepper; brown quickly in oil. Reduce heat, add onion, and simmer 3 to 4 hours, slowly adding beer at intervals. Roast should be loosely covered.

Before serving, skim fat and stir sour cream into pan juices, mixing well.

*Serves up to 8.*

## BOILED BEEF AND BEER

5 *pounds beef rump or flank*     2 *bay leaves*
*Salt and pepper*     3 *slices lemon rind*
6 *slices bacon*     6 *juniper berries*
2 *onions*     2 *12-ounce cans beer*
2 *carrots*     2 *tablespoons butter*
2 *turnips*     2 *tablespoons flour*
6 *peppercorns*

Pound beef with a wooden mallet and rub it well with salt and pepper. Place in a deep, oven-proof casserole on a bed of bacon slices. Chop onions, carrots, and turnips into small, even pieces and spread over and around meat. Add to chopped vegetables peppercorns, bay leaves, lemon rind, and berries. Add just enough beer to cover meat. (The quantity indicated may or may not be sufficient; it's all according to the size of the casserole.)

Cover casserole and simmer 2½ hours. Drain off reduced

broth and set aside 2 cups of it. Brown 2 tablespoons butter and blend in flour. Stir and cook until roux is brown and smooth. Gradually add 2 cups of broth from meat and simmer over very low heat 20 minutes. Add salt and pepper to taste. Pour sauce over beef and serve from casserole. *Serves 6 to 8.*

## OLD WORLD RIBS

3–4 *pounds lean beef*
   *short ribs*
3 *tablespoons flour*
1 *teaspoon paprika*
1 *teaspoon salt*

⅛ *teaspoon pepper*
1 *8-ounce can tomato sauce*
   *with onions*
1 *cup beer*
1 *teaspoon caraway seeds*

Coat ribs with mixture of flour and seasonings. Arrange in single layer in shallow baking dish (try not to let them touch each other). Bake at 500° 25 minutes. Pour off fat.

Mix tomato sauce and beer with caraway seeds and pour over ribs. Reduce oven to 325° and bake 1 to 1½ hours.

The drippings may be skimmed of fat and poured over 2 cups of cooked wide noodles.
*Serves 4 to 6.*

## SHISH KEBAB

1 *cup beer*
¼ *cup salad oil*
1 *medium onion, diced*
2 *teaspoons curry powder*
1 *teaspoon ginger*
¼ *teaspoon garlic powder*
1 *tablespoon salt*

2½ *pounds beef, cut into*
   *2-inch chunks*
1 *pound whole mushrooms*
2 *green peppers, cut into*
   *squares*
2 *onions, sliced*

Mix beer, salad oil, and onion with seasonings. Pour over

beef squares and marinate at least 4 hours (or overnight) in covered dish in refrigerator.

Thread on skewers, alternating with mushroom crowns, green pepper squares, and onion slices. Roast, basting with marinade, or grill over hot coals, turning frequently and basting.

*Serves 4 to 5.*

## AUTUMN GOULASH

| | |
|---|---|
| 2 *pounds lean beef, cubed* | 1½ *tablespoons flour* |
| ½ *teaspoon salt* | 1 *12-ounce can beer* |
| ¼ *teaspoon pepper* | ½ *cup chicken bouillon* |
| 2 *teaspoons butter* | 1 *teaspoon Dijon mustard* |
| 2 *tablespoons peanut oil* | 1 *teaspoon caraway seeds* |
| 2 *cups thinly sliced onions* | 1 *cup sour cream* |
| 2 *tablespoons paprika* | |

Sprinkle beef with salt and pepper. Melt butter and oil together in a large skillet and brown beef on all sides. Transfer to a heavy casserole.

Add onions to skillet and cook until wilted. Sprinkle paprika and flour over onions and stir in liquids, mixing well. Add mustard and caraway seeds and bring to boil. Pour onion mixture over beef. Cover and bake at 350° 1 to 1½ hours.

Stir in sour cream just before serving. If necessary, add more salt to taste. This is great over noodles.

*Serves 6.*

## SURPRISE BURGERS

| | |
|---|---|
| 2 *pounds ground chuck* | ½ *cup beer* |
| ½ *medium onion, finely chopped* | *Salt and pepper* |

Mix ground meat lightly with onion. Heat a heavy skillet

or electric frying pan. Form meat into 6 large or 8 medium patties; place patties in skillet. Using a large spoon, make an indentation in the top of each and fill with beer. Sprinkle salt and pepper over patties. When first side is cooked, beer will be absorbed. Turn and brown other side.

*Serves 8.*

## MUSHROOM MEATBALLS

This is a quick dish to prepare!

1½ *pounds ground round*
1 *teaspoon salt*
½ *teaspoon pepper*
1 *tablespoon Worcestershire*
  *sauce*
¼ *teaspoon garlic powder*
2 *cans cream of mushroom*
  *soup*
2 *12-ounce cans beer*
½ *pound fresh mushrooms*
  *(or 1 large can)*

Mix together ground beef, salt, pepper, Worcestershire sauce, and garlic powder. Form into balls and fry quickly until brown. Dilute cream of mushroom soup with beer instead of milk. Fill empty soup can twice to measure beer. Blend and set aside.

Add mushrooms to meatballs and cook 5 minutes. Add soup mixture and simmer 15 minutes.

*Serves 4 to 6.*

## CURRIED BEEF STROGANOFF BALLS

2 *pounds ground beef*
1 *cup beer*
½ *teaspoon curry powder*
⅓ *cup minced onion*
2 *teaspoons salt*
½ *teaspoon Tabasco sauce*
2 *eggs*
1 *cup bread crumbs*
2 *tablespoons butter*
1 *6-ounce can mushrooms*
1 *clove garlic*
2 *tablespoons flour*
1 *cup sour cream*

Mix ground beef, ½ cup beer, curry powder, onion, salt, Tabasco sauce, eggs, and bread crumbs; shape into meatballs.

Brown meatballs in butter, and add mushrooms with liquid from can, remaining beer, and garlic. Simmer 10 minutes. Remove garlic, blend in flour, and stir until smooth. Gently fold in sour cream and heat over low heat until almost bubbling.

This dish goes well with buttered noodles.

*Serves 8.*

## NORDIC MEATBALLS

| | |
|---|---|
| 1 *pound lean ground beef* | 1 *tablespoon flour* |
| ½ *pound pork sausage meat* | 1½ *cups beer* |
| ¼ *cup chopped onion* | 1 *clove garlic, crushed* |
| 1 *egg, lightly beaten* | ½ *cup canned tomato puree* |
| 1 *teaspoon salt* | 1 *teaspoon crushed dried dill* |
| *Pepper to taste* | 1 *cup stuffed green olives* |
| 1 *tablespoon cooking oil* | |

Combine meats, onion, egg, salt, and pepper, and shape into small balls. Heat oil in a heavy skillet or electric frying pan. Brown meatballs on all sides; remove from pan.

Stir in flour and gradually add beer, cooking and stirring until thick and smooth. Return meatballs to sauce and add remaining ingredients, except olives. Cover skillet and simmer 10 minutes. Add olives and cook another 2 minutes.

Serve over buttered broad noodles or cooked rice.

*Serves 4.*

## MATCHLESS MEAT LOAF

½ cup beer
3 slices bread, toasted
1½ pounds lean ground
  beef
½ pound ground pork
½ teaspoon chopped garlic

1 teaspoon black pepper
1 tablespoon salt
¼ cup chopped onions
4 tablespoons chopped
  celery
1 egg, slightly beaten

Pour beer over bread and set aside. Mix meats together, add seasonings, onions, celery, and egg, and toss lightly. Add bread mixture. Place in loaf pan or shape into loaf in roasting pan.

Preheat oven to 375° and bake loaf 45 minutes to 1 hour.

*Serves 6 to 8.*


## SAVORY MEAT LOAF

1 egg
1 cup beer
1 cup soft bread crumbs
¾ teaspoon salt
¼ teaspoon pepper

1 tablespoon dried onion
  flakes
½ teaspoon thyme
1 pound ground beef
2 tablespoons butter
⅓ cup chili sauce

In a large bowl beat egg slightly, then add ⅓ cup beer, bread crumbs, and seasonings. Mix thoroughly with meat and shape into a loaf.

Melt butter in a skillet and brown meat loaf on both sides. Add remaining beer, cover, and simmer 20 minutes. Stir in chili sauce, heat through again, and serve.

*Serves 4.*

## KIELBASA AND BEER

2 *pounds kielbasa (Polish
    sausage)*
1 *12-ounce can beer*
2 *tablespoons instant minced
    onions*
1 *bay leaf*

¼ *teaspoon pepper*
1 *14-ounce package
    macaroni-and-cheese
    dinner*
1 *tablespoon chopped
    parsley*

Cut sausage into chunks, then brown lightly in a large
skillet over high heat. Add beer, onion, bay leaf, and pepper.
Simmer 10 minutes.

Prepare macaroni and cheese as directed on package and
place on a warm platter. Drain sausage and place around
macaroni. Top with parsley.

*Serves 4 to 6.*

## FRANKFURTERS AND SAUERKRAUT

2 *pounds sauerkraut*
1 *12-ounce can beer*
1 *small onion, chopped*
1 *tablespoon butter*
1 *marrowbone, cracked*
10 *peppercorns*

1 *tart apple, peeled and
    sliced*
3 *tablespoons sherry*
2 *pounds frankfurters*
2 *cups light ale*
¼ *teaspoon brown sugar*
2 *cloves*

Drain sauerkraut well and wash under cold water. Drain
again. Place in a heavy saucepan with enough beer to
cover. Sauté onion in butter and add to sauerkraut. Then
add marrowbone, peppercorns, and apple to sauerkraut and
simmer covered 2 hours. When done, add sherry. Stir.

In boiling water cook frankfurters 5 minutes and drain.

Add ale, brown sugar, and cloves; cover. Steam 10 minutes.

Serve frankfurters and heaping portions of sauerkraut with crispy buttered rolls.

*Serves 6 to 8.*

## KNOCKWURST IN BEER

4 *knockwursts*      1 *tablespoon vinegar*
½ *cup beer*      ½ *teaspoon sugar*

In a covered saucepan, simmer knockwursts in beer 15 minutes. Place knockwursts in shallow, warm, heatproof serving dish. Keep hot.

Boil up pan liquid, reduce to ¼ cup, and stir in vinegar and sugar. Pour over hot knockwursts.

Serve with mashed potatoes and red cabbage, or hot sauerkraut sprinkled with caraway seeds.

*Serves 4.*

## LAGERED KRAUT AND WURSTS

1 *quart sauerkraut*      6–8 *knockwursts*
1 *16-ounce can beer*      ¼ *teaspoon pepper*

Pour sauerkraut in beer and cook covered over low flame 1 hour.

Place a layer of sauerkraut in a casserole. Add knockwursts and cover with remaining sauerkraut and juice. Sprinkle with pepper. Cover and bake at 350° 1 hour. Add more beer if necessary.

*Serves 6 hearty portions.*

## SWEDISH STEW

¼ pound salt pork, diced
1 pound boneless stewing
  beef, cubed
1 pound beef heart, diced
¼ cup flour, seasoned with
  1 teaspoon salt
4 onions, sliced
4–6 potatoes, sliced thick

2 cups diced rutabaga
Salt and pepper to taste
¼ cup tomato catsup
1 12-ounce can beer
1 cup bouillon (or bouillon
  cube and water)
1 bay leaf

Heat salt pork in a heavy pot to draw out fat. Dredge beef and heart in flour.

Brown meat in pork fat, removing meat as it browns. Place half of it in a layer on bottom of heavy casserole. Add vegetables in layers, sprinkling each layer with salt and pepper. Place remaining meat on top. Mix catsup and beer together and pour over meat. Add bouillon and bay leaf. Cover tightly and simmer 1½ to 2 hours.

*Serves 6 to 8.*

## GERMAN BEEF ROLL-UPS

2 pounds round steak
Salt and pepper to taste
4 slices bacon
1 onion, sliced
1 tablespoon dark corn syrup
½ cup vinegar

2 cloves
2 bay leaves
2 peppercorns
1 teaspoon caraway seeds
Beer
Water

Have butcher cut beef into 4 slices. Season each slice with salt and pepper, then roll up and tie securely. Place strips of bacon in bottom of a casserole, then place onion slices on top of bacon and beef rolls on top of onion slices. Add corn syrup, vinegar, cloves, bay leaves, peppercorns, and caraway seeds.

Use equal parts of beer and water to cover meat. (About 1 cup each should do it, but it does depend on the size and shape of your casserole.) Cover and bake at 350° 2 hours, or until tender. Before serving, remove excess fat from sauce and pour sauce over roll-ups.

This dish is excellent with boiled potatoes and ice-cold beer.

*Serves 4.*

## SAUERBRATEN WITH BEER

| | |
|---|---|
| 2 cups white vinegar | 1 teaspoon peppercorns |
| 1⅓ cups beer | ½ teaspoon pepper |
| ⅔ cup water | 4 pounds beef brisket, |
| 2 onions, sliced | trimmed of all fat |
| 1 orange, peeled and sliced | 2 tablespoons oil |
| 1 clove garlic, minced | ¼ cup tomato puree |
| 1 bay leaf | 2 tablespoons softened |
| 1 tablespoon salt | butter |
| 1 teaspoon whole cloves | 3 tablespoons flour |

Combine vinegar, beer, water, onions, orange slices, garlic, bay leaf, salt, cloves, peppercorns, and pepper in a bowl. Set brisket in bowl and refrigerate, covered, 5 days, stirring the marinade and turning the meat once each day.

After 5 days, strain marinade and drain meat well. Reserve onion slices.

In a large pan, brown the meat on all sides in oil. Add strained marinade, reserved onion slices, and tomato puree.

Cook uncovered, for about 2½ hours, or until very tender.

Mix softened butter and flour together in a small bowl. Gradually add the butter-flour mixture to gravy in pan, stirring until thickened. Cook over low flame at least 8 minutes longer, until smooth. Serve the sauerbraten with the gravy.

*Serves 6 to 8.*

## GERMAN VEAL CHOPS

For real old-time flavor, we can't rave enough about this easy and quick-to-make veal dish. It's enticingly spiced and different too!

| | |
|---|---|
| *4 veal cutlets (or chops)* | *1 cup dark beer or ale* |
| *Salt and pepper to taste* | *1 bay leaf* |
| *1 tablespoon butter* | *2 tablespoons flour* |
| *2 medium onions, sliced* | |

Sprinkle meat with salt and pepper and brown lightly in butter on both sides. Add onions and a little more butter and cook a few more minutes. Add beer and bay leaf and simmer 15 minutes, or until done.

Make a paste of flour and a little extra beer; stir into pan juices and cook until sauce is slightly thickened.

This goes well with buttered parsley potatoes and ice-cold ale.

*Serves 4.*

## TONGUE IN BEER

Beef tongue is usually served cold as part of a platter of assorted cold meats. We found this a unique and tasty

innovation that is economical and different. Try it and hear
your family cry for more!

1 *fresh or pickled tongue*  1 *tablespoon whole pickling*
  *(about 4 pounds)*  *spice*
2 *cups beer*

Place tongue in a deep saucepan; add beer. If this does not
cover the meat entirely, add cold water to cover. Place
pickling spice in liquid and cover. Bring to boil, lower heat,
and simmer 2½ hours, or until tender.

Remove tongue and cool slightly. Trim off any fat and
gristle and remove skin by slashing underside with a paring
knife. Turn tongue and grasp skin at the thick end and pull.
Skin should come off easily.

Slice in ½-inch-thick pieces. Set aside and keep warm while
you prepare Apple-Raisin Sauce.

*Serves 6.*

## Apple-Raisin Sauce

4 *tablespoons butter*  2 *tablespoons cider vinegar*
¼ *cup flour*  2 *tablespoons brown sugar*
1¼ *cups apple juice*  ½ *cup raisins*
¾ *cup beer*

In a small saucepan melt butter, then stir in flour. Gradually
add apple juice and beer, stirring constantly. Add vinegar,
sugar, and raisins and simmer over low heat until smooth
and slightly thick.

Place slices of tongue on a warm platter and pour hot sauce
over it. Serve immediately.

# Pork

One of the most versatile meats is pork; one seldom tires of it because its appearance and taste can so easily be changed. However, it must be well done. Our first recipe, Spicy Pork Chops, has a tasteful richness that would be appropriate for a dinner party.

Bavarian Casserole is a magic way to use a leftover roast, but you can also try it with a canned pork shoulder. We don't think you can beat this dish for speed, low cost, and zingy flavor!

It will certainly lift your spirits and not your pocketbook if you take a short time to plan your menus with imagination before you take that weekly trip to the market. For starters, perhaps a Pilsnered Pork Roast and Dressing for Sunday, and leftovers frozen for a casserole on Wednesday, is one suggestion. You take it from there and make it your own!

# Pork

## SPICY PORK CHOPS

8 *tablespoons butter*
6 *loin pork chops*
*Salt and pepper*
6 *large onions, sliced*
1 *tablespoon flour*

1 *12-ounce can beer*
*Bouquet garni*
1 *teaspoon brown sugar*
*Chopped parsley*

Heat 4 tablespoons butter in a heavy skillet or electric frying pan and quickly brown chops. Season with salt and pepper. Set aside on a warm platter. Use remaining amount of butter and gently sauté onions, then sprinkle with flour, and stir well. Cook 5 minutes. Add half the amount of beer and bring to boil, stirring constantly. Set aside.

Make a bouquet garni using 1 bay leaf, 6 parsley sprigs, and ½ teaspoon thyme tied in cheesecloth (or use 1 teaspoon dried, ready-mixed bouquet garni). Return chops to skillet with bouquet garni and sprinkle brown sugar over tops of chops. Pour remaining beer and onion mixture (add more beer if necessary) to cover chops. Bring to boil, cover, and simmer 1 hour. Serve in a deep platter and sprinkle with parsley.

*Serves 6.*

## HONEYED SPARERIBS

8 *pounds spareribs*
3 *cups beer*
1 *cup honey*
1½ *teaspoons dry mustard*
2 *teaspoons chili powder*

2 *teaspoons finely crumbled*
  *sage*
4 *tablespoons horseradish*
1 *tablespoon salt*
2 *tablespoons lemon juice*

Place ribs in a large, shallow pan. Mix remaining ingredients for marinade and pour over ribs. Let stand 2 to 4 hours, turning at least once.

To cook, remove ribs from marinade (save marinade) and weave them on a spit or long skewers. Or, place flat on rack of hot outdoor grill about 4 inches from coals. Cook until brown, turning frequently and brushing with marinade each time.

*Serves 8 hearty appetites!*

## BEER-GLAZED HAM OR PORK LOIN

1 *precooked boned ham or pork loin (Canadian bacon is also excellent)*
½ *cup beer*

½ *cup brown sugar*
1 *teaspoon dry mustard*
1 *teaspoon ground cloves*

Preheat oven to 325°. Heat ham or loin ½ hour.

Combine remaining ingredients and spoon mixture over warm meat. Return to oven for an additional 30 minutes, basting frequently, until glazed.

*Serves 4 to 6.*

## BAVARIAN PORK CHOPS AND SAUERKRAUT

2 *pounds sauerkraut*
4 *cups beer*
6 *large pork chops*
1½ *teaspoons salt*

1 *teaspoon black pepper*
2 *cloves garlic, minced*
1½ *cups chopped apple*
1½ *cups grated potato*

Wash sauerkraut and combine with 2 cups beer in a saucepan. Cook over low heat 2 hours, stirring frequently.

Season pork chops with half the required amounts of salt and pepper, and brown.

# Pork

Spread half the sauerkraut on the bottom of a casserole. Sprinkle with remaining salt and pepper and then the garlic. Arrange pork chops over sauerkraut. Spread apples and potatoes over pork chops and cover with remaining sauerkraut and beer. Cover and bake at 350° approximately 45 minutes, or until chops are tender.

*Serves 6.*

## PILSNERED PORK ROAST AND DRESSING

4-*pound pork roast*
½ *teaspoon garlic salt*
½ *teaspoon onion salt*
¼ *teaspoon rosemary*
*Salt and pepper*
1 *cup pilsner beer*

1¼ *tablespoons brown sugar*
1 *tablespoon lemon juice*
1 *tablespoon prepared mustard*
1 *tablespoon Worcestershire sauce*

Preheat oven to 400°. Rub seasonings on roast and bake ½ hour. Combine remaining ingredients and pour over meat. Bake roast for 1 additional hour, basting often. Prepare Cornbread Dressing (see below).

Place Cornbread Dressing around meat and continue baking at 350° until done. Total cooking time, approximately 3 hours. Serve with gravy described (see page 67).

*Serves 6 man-sized appetites.*

### Cornbread Dressing

4 *cups prepared cornbread dressing*
1 *cup beer (or more) to moisten dressing*

Lightly mix together.

### Gravy

½ cup roast liquid
1½ cups water

½ package dried mushroom
  soup mix

Combine and boil until thick.

## BAVARIAN CASSEROLE

A good recipe for using up leftover pork, and so delicious!

¼ cup chopped onion
¼ cup chopped celery
2 tablespoons butter
3 cups cubed cooked pork
1 cup beer

1½ cups pumpernickel
  bread crumbs
¼ teaspoon sugar
1 teaspoon salt
¼ teaspoon coarse black
  pepper

Sauté onion and celery in butter until soft and yellow. Add cubed pork and stir. Mix beer and remaining ingredients together and place in a casserole. Cover and bake at 375° 40 minutes.

*Serves 6.*

## SAUCY SAUSAGES

So good for a surprise Sunday supper.

1 pound pork sausage
1 cup beer
1 bay leaf

3 peppercorns
1 clove

Brown sausage and remove fat. Mix in beer and seasonings. Bring to boil, then cover and simmer 20 minutes.

*Serves 4.*

## BEER-BRAISED PORK

3 pounds fresh pork
   shoulder
3 pounds onions
6 tablespoons butter

1 bay leaf
½ teaspoon thyme
1 pint beer

Cut pork into 2-inch cubes and brown quickly in a skillet. Slice onions and lightly sauté in butter. Remove onions from butter and mix with meat. Add bay leaf, thyme, and beer. Cover and simmer 1½ to 2 hours.

Serve with boiled potatoes and cole slaw.

*Serves 6.*

## BAKED FRESH HAM

We found this old-time favorite with a new twist. It's luscious dining and perfect for a large, informal gathering.

¼ cup soy sauce
¼ cup honey
¾ cup beer
2 tablespoons sherry

2 teaspoons salt
½ teaspoon ground ginger
1 9-pound fresh ham
10 small apples, unpeeled

Blend soy sauce, honey, beer, sherry, salt, and ginger for marinade. Brush all sides of ham with marinade and let stand overnight in refrigerator, or at least 4 hours (turning often and moistening frequently).

Preheat oven to 350° and roast (allowing 35 minutes per pound) 3 hours and 15 minutes, basting frequently. An hour before cooking time is up, add apples to roast (on rack, not in pan liquid) and baste.

*Serves 15.*

## GREEK LAMB-MEATBALLS

We don't have a lamb chapter but this recipe is both economical and nourishing, and the taste is so intriguing we just had to include it! Grecian-inspired, it's a blending of ground lamb, cracked wheat, yogurt, spices, and bouillon, simmered in beer. Perfect beer-eating down to the last morsel, it's a masterpiece you must try.

| | |
|---|---|
| 1 *pound ground lamb* | ¼ *teaspoon cinnamon* |
| ½ *cup cracked wheat\** | 2 *cups chicken bouillon* |
| 1 *medium onion, minced* | 1 *12-ounce can beer or ale* |
| 1 *egg, well beaten* | ¼ *cup melted butter* |
| 1 *teaspoon salt* | ¼ *cup flour* |
| ½ *teaspoon ground* | 1 *cup yogurt* |
| *coriander* | 1 *tablespoon dried dill weed* |

Combine lamb, cracked wheat, onion, egg, salt, coriander, and cinnamon. Mix well and shape into meatballs. In a saucepan, blend bouillon and beer. Heat. Add meatballs and simmer 20 minutes, turning occasionally.

Meanwhile, in another pan, blend butter with flour, adding a little water to make a paste. Gradually add just a little of the hot bouillon-beer mixture, and stir. Pour this entire mixture into the saucepan with the meatballs and cook, stirring until smooth. Simmer 5 minutes. Remove from heat and stir in yogurt and dill weed.

This dish is excellent with rice and tall glasses of pilsner beer.

*Serves 4 to 6.*

---

\* *Note:* If not in your local supermarket, cracked wheat is usually found in specialty-food stores and health-food stores.

# Chicken

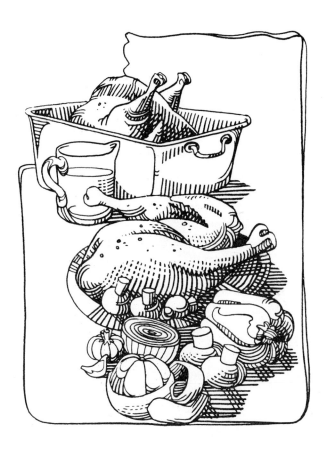

**E**very poet and dramatist through the ages has written about poultry and the elegant fowl. From the early times of the Romans, who are credited with popularizing poultry in Europe, onward to Henri IV, who promised the working man a Poulet-au-Pot, the virtues of chicken have been proclaimed. We can't begin to compete with the poets' meticulous devotion to the beauty of the honored bird. However, we shall try to compete with some tasty dishes of merit—all with beer included.

## BAKED BEER CHICKEN

½ cup steak sauce
¼ cup Worcestershire sauce
2 cups beer
1 tablespoon pepper
1 tablespoon salt

2 cloves garlic, minced
2 small broilers, split in half
½ cup oil
½ cup catsup

Combine all ingredients except oil and catsup. In a shallow baking dish marinate chicken overnight in refrigerator (or minimum of 6 hours).

Drain chickens. Remove marinade to a small bowl and blend in oil and catsup. Return chickens to baking dish and brush with marinade. Bake at 325° 1 hour, basting frequently. This is also excellent cooked on an outdoor grill.

*Serves 4.*

## CHICKEN IN BEER WITH RICE #1

2 3-pound chickens,
   quartered
2 teaspoons salt
½ teaspoon pepper
1 teaspoon paprika
¼ cup peanut oil
¾ pound ham, cut in bite-
   size pieces

2 large onions, chopped
3 cups water
1 pint beer
½ teaspoon saffron
4 chicken bouillon cubes
3 cups long grain rice
2 cans drained peas

Wash chicken pieces, pat dry, and sprinkle with salt, pepper, and paprika. In a skillet, brown well in oil; place in a casserole. Fry ham 3 to 4 minutes and place in casserole. Sauté onion until clear and add to chicken and ham.

Rinse skillet with 3 cups water and add to casserole with

beer, saffron, and bouillon cubes. Add rice and stir. Bake at 350° ½ hour. Stir with fork, tossing rice. Add peas, cover, and bake 15 minutes more.

*Serves 8.*

## CHICKEN IN BEER WITH RICE #2

| | |
|---|---|
| 2 3-pound fryers | Salt and pepper to taste |
| Oil | 2 cups chicken stock |
| 3 fresh, hot red peppers | 2 cups rice |
| 6 large cloves garlic | 2 cups beer |
| 1 large onion | ½ cup frozen green peas |
| 1 teaspoon ground cumin seed | Cherry tomatoes and hot red peppers, as garnish |

Cut chicken into serving pieces and brown lightly on all sides in very small amount of oil. Remove to a heavy casserole. Seed the red peppers and grind. Crush garlic cloves and chop onion very fine. Sauté peppers, garlic, and onion in remaining fat only until onion is golden. Add this mixture to chicken along with cumin seed and salt and pepper to taste. Add chicken stock to cover chicken (2 cups may not be necessary). Cover.

Cook over low heat 45 minutes. Strain off liquid and measure it. Again, you need 2 cups of stock. If chicken liquid isn't enough, add more stock to make 2 cups. Along with these 2 cups of liquid, add rice and beer to casserole. Cover and cook until rice is tender.

Mix in peas and let stand covered 5 minutes. Heat will cook frozen peas.

Garnish with cherry tomatoes and hot red peppers.

*Serves 6 to 8.*

## CHARCOAL CHICKEN

2 *broilers, cut into serving*
  *pieces*
¼ *cup cider vinegar*
¼ *cup Worcestershire sauce*
¼ *pound margarine*
1 *medium onion, finely*
  *chopped*
2 *cloves garlic, minced*

1 *teaspoon dry mustard*
1 *tablespoon celery seed*
1 *teaspoon sugar*
1 *teaspoon salt*
1 *teaspoon pepper*
1 *cup beer*
1 *bottle catsup*

Place chicken pieces on foil over charcoal fire. Combine all other ingredients in a saucepan and bring to boil over low heat. Stir and simmer 5 minutes, then use to baste chicken. Turn chicken every 5 minutes, basting frequently until done.

*Serves 6.*

## SPANISH CHICKEN

½ *cup cooking oil*
1 *fryer, cut into serving*
  *pieces*
1 *green pepper, chopped*
1 *clove garlic, minced*
2 *medium onions, chopped*

½ *teaspoon paprika*
1 *teaspoon salt*
1 *8-ounce can tomato sauce*
1 *cup chicken broth*
1½ *cups beer*
1 *cup raw rice*

In a heavy skillet, heat oil and brown chicken pieces. Remove chicken and simmer green pepper, garlic, and onions in remaining oil.

Replace chicken and add all other ingredients except rice. Cover and simmer 20 minutes. Add rice and continue simmering until rice is done.

*Serves 4.*

## CHICKEN FLEMISH STYLE

1 3½-pound broiler, cut into serving pieces
1 cup butter
3 large onions, finely chopped
⅓ cup white vinegar
1 tablespoon sugar
½ teaspoon prepared mustard
4 slices bread
1 tablespoon dried bouquet garni
1 quart beer
Salt and pepper to taste

In a frying pan, brown chicken well in ¾ cup butter. In a large casserole, in which you will be cooking chicken, sauté onions in ¼ cup butter and add vinegar and sugar. Add chicken pieces to onion mixture in casserole.

Spread mustard on the bread slices and place them evenly around in the casserole. Sprinkle dried bouquet garni over entire contents and pour in enough beer to cover. (It may be less than the entire quart.) Season with salt and pepper, and cover. Cook over low flame until chicken is tender (about 45 minutes to 1 hour).

*Serves 4.*

## CURRIED CREAMED CHICKEN

This is a quickie for when you're in a rush, or when you have leftover chicken and want to be different.

½ teaspoon curry powder
½ cup beer
2 tablespoons chili sauce
1 can cream of mushroom soup, undiluted
1 cup diced leftover chicken

Blend curry powder, beer, chili sauce, and soup. Heat thoroughly. Add chicken, stir, and simmer 3 minutes.

Serve with rice or buttered noodles.

*Serves 2.*

## SKILLET CHICKEN

1 *fryer, cut up into eighths*
¼ *cup oil*
1 *clove garlic, minced*
1 *onion, finely chopped*
1½ *teaspoons salt*
1 *teaspoon pepper*

½ *green pepper, diced*
½ *cup beer*
1 *4-ounce can mushrooms*
1 *cup canned Italian
   tomatoes*

Sauté chicken in oil in a large skillet. Add garlic, onion, seasonings, and green pepper. Cook 5 minutes. Add beer and simmer covered 20 minutes. Add mushrooms and tomatoes; cover, and cook another 15 minutes.

Rice is a *must*!

*Serves 4.*

## ORANGERIE CHICKEN

1 *fryer, cut into serving
   pieces*
⅔ *cup orange juice*
1 *orange rind, cut into strips*

⅔ *cup currant jelly*
½ *cup beer*
1 *tablespoon cornstarch*
1 *tablespoon beer*

Broil chicken and set aside.

Combine orange juice, orange rind strips, jelly, and ½ cup beer in a saucepan. Simmer 15 minutes.

Dissolve cornstarch in 1 tablespoon beer and add to orange juice mixture. Simmer until thickened, stirring constantly. Place broiled chicken on a heated platter and pour orange sauce on top.

*Serves 4.*

# Fish

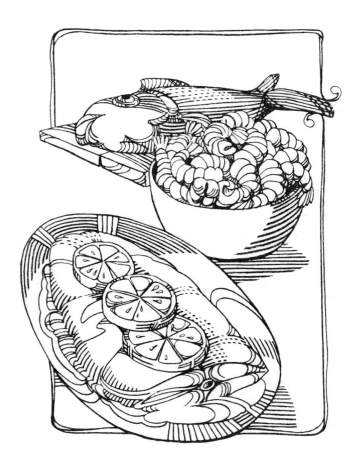

**F**ish and beer are as compatible as ham and eggs. Some fish and beer recipes, we've been told, go back to 1612, when the Dutch West India Company built its first brewery in Manhattan.

We know that beer played an important part in colonial life. Many farms grew their own barley and brewed beer at home. You will find the friendly combinations of fish and beer distinctive. The beer points up the flavor of the fish and other ingredients, and the cereal content in beer seems to soften any strong "fishy" or "fish-oil" taste.

Always try to use fresh fish for your dishes. However, today most supermarkets carry fine varieties of frozen fish that do very well if you don't live near a fresh-fish market. In any case, with all of the recipes we have in this chapter, please don't overcook!

## BATTER FOR FRYING FISH

| | |
|---|---|
| 1 cup flour | ¼ teaspoon pepper |
| 8 ounces beer | ½ teaspoon salt |

Blend all ingredients together. Dip fish into batter and fry in hot oil or vegetable shortening.

*Makes 2 cups.*

## BEER FISH FRY

| | |
|---|---|
| 2 eggs, separated | 3 tablespoons melted |
| ⅔ cup beer | margarine |
| 1 cup flour | 1½–2 pounds cod fillets (or |
| ¾ teaspoon salt | haddock, or flounder) |
| | Hot fat |

Beat egg yolks and beer together. Gently stir in flour and salt until blended. Mix in margarine and allow to stand at room temperature 30 minutes. Beat egg whites until stiff and fold into flour mixture. Dip fish pieces into mixture and drop into preheated deep hot fat. Cook until lightly browned, then remove fish and drain on paper towels. Serve immediately.

*Serves 6.*

## BAKED FILLET OF SOLE

| | |
|---|---|
| 2 pounds grey sole fillets | 2 tablespoons butter |
| 1 12-ounce can ale | 2 tablespoons flour |
| ½ teaspoon celery seeds | ½ cup ale (if needed) |
| 1 onion, chopped | ½ cup sour cream |
| ¼ teaspoon ginger | ¼ teaspoon paprika |
| ½ teaspoon caraway seeds | |

Bake fillets in a buttered baking dish with ale and seasonings at 350° 20 minutes.

In a saucepan melt butter, then stir in flour until golden. Pour liquid from baking dish into a cup and add enough ale to measure a full cup. Add to flour mixture and stir well until smooth and thickened. Fold in sour cream and pour sauce over fillets. Sprinkle with paprika and put under broiler 3 minutes, or until golden brown and hot.

*Serves 4.*

## SOLE WITH SHELLFISH

We found this ideal for Sunday buffets. It can be made early in the day and refrigerated until you're ready to bake. However, do let it stand at room temperature for an hour before you put it in a preheated 350° oven.

20 *serving-size pieces of*
   *fillet of sole*
*Salt and pepper to taste*
⅔ *cup butter*
5 *tablespoons sifted flour*
1 *cup chicken broth*
½ *cup beer*
½ *pound small cooked*
   *shrimp*

½ *can crabmeat*
½ *teaspoon Tabasco sauce*
2 *tablespoons Worcestershire*
   *sauce*
½ *teaspoon paprika*
½ *cup grated Parmesan*
   *cheese*

Sprinkle fillets with salt and pepper. Oil a large casserole and carefully space out fillets in two layers, so that there are 10 portions. Bake at 350° 20 minutes.

Melt ½ cup butter and add flour, stirring constantly. Let mixture become golden. Drain liquid from casserole and add enough chicken broth to make 2½ cups liquid. Stir liquid into flour mixture and cook until smooth and thickened. Stir well. Add beer, shrimp, crabmeat, Tabasco, and Worcestershire sauce. Dot fillets with remaining butter, pour sauce over fish. Sprinkle with paprika and Parmesan cheese. Bake uncovered at 350° 25 minutes, or until bubbling.

*Serves 10.*

## BAKED HERRING IN BEER

If you're fortunate enough to live near or in New England, fresh herring should be available most of the year. They're especially plentiful from April through the end of spring. Fresh herring (or alewives, as naturalists call them) are not always at the local market, so their cousin, shad, may be substituted in this hearty, full-flavored dish.

10 *fresh herrings*              1 *medium onion*
½ *teaspoon allspice*        ¾ *cup beer*
½ *teaspoon ground cloves*   ¾ *cup vinegar*
*Salt and pepper*

Have fish cleaned and heads and tails removed. Wash and drain thoroughly. Arrange in a shallow baking dish and sprinkle with seasonings. Slice onion over fish. Pour beer and vinegar into dish, making sure liquid almost covers fish. Cover and bake at 450° 25 minutes, or until done.

*Serves 6 to 8 (according to size of fish and appetites).*

## BEER-BAKED BASS

Since the size of fish varies, we leave the exact number of pounds up to you. Allow about two servings per pound. (The usual bass serves 4 to 5.)

1 *large baking-size bass*
*Salt and pepper to taste*
⅓ *cup olive oil*
1 *onion, chopped*
½ *cup chopped parsley*
1 *clove garlic, finely*
   *chopped*

1 *cup canned tomatoes,*
   *chopped*
½ *teaspoon tomato paste*
¼ *teaspoon oregano*
½ *cup beer*

Place fish in a shallow baking dish. Season with salt and pepper. Sprinkle oil evenly over top and place in 350° oven until oil is hot. Add onion, parsley, and garlic.

Meanwhile mix tomatoes, tomato paste, oregano, and beer together. When onions are brown, add tomato mixture to top of fish and continue baking 30 minutes, or until fish flakes easily.

*Serves 4.*

## POACHED SWORDFISH STEAKS
## WITH CHEESE SAUCE

1 *small carrot*
1 *small stalk celery*
1 *medium onion*
2 *cups beer*
2 *sprigs parsley*

1 *small bay leaf*
2 *whole cloves*
4 *peppercorns*
4 *swordfish steaks*

Slice carrot, celery, and onion. Place beer, vegetables, and seasonings in large skillet. Bring to a boil, then cover and simmer 15 minutes.

Arrange swordfish steaks in broth; cover and simmer about 10 minutes. Turn fish once. Fish should flake easily when tested with a fork. Transfer fish to a greased baking dish. Reserve broth. Prepare Cheese Sauce (see page 86).

*Serves 4.*

## Cheese Sauce

Fish broth (from
  preceding recipe)
1½ tablespoons butter
1 tablespoon flour
½ cup milk
⅓ cup Gruyère cheese

¼ cup grated Parmesan
  cheese
1 egg yolk
2 tablespoons cream
¼ teaspoon salt
¼ teaspoon pepper

Rapidly boil fish broth until reduced to ½ cup. Strain through cheesecloth.

Melt ¾ tablespoon butter, add flour, and blend with a wire whisk. Bring milk to a boil and add to above, stirring constantly until sauce is smooth and thickened. Add the strained broth and cheeses and mix carefully.

Lightly beat egg yolk and add small amount of hot sauce. Add to above mixture and cook over low heat until sauce has thickened. Stir in rest of butter, cream, and seasonings. Pour sauce over fish and broil until lightly browned.

## HAWAIIAN SHRIMP KABOBS

4 slices bacon
2 pounds fried shrimp
  (Double Fried Shrimp
  recipe shown on p. 88)

1 20-ounce can pineapple
  chunks
1 6-ounce can whole
  mushrooms

Partially cook bacon; cut each slice into 4 pieces. On skewers, alternate cooked shrimp, bacon, pineapple chunks, and mushrooms. This may be done in advance. Just prior to serving, place kabobs under broiler just to heat shrimps through.

Serve on a bed of rice with a sweet and pungent sauce.

*Serves 6 hearty appetites.*

## LOIS FENTON'S BAR-B-QUED SHRIMP

1½ *pounds raw shrimp*
⅛ *cup melted butter*
⅛ *cup olive oil*
2 *tablespoons Worcestershire*
   *sauce*
6 *tablespoons catsup*

*Juice of 1 lemon*
6 *tablespoons beer*
¼ *teaspoon salt*
¼ *teaspoon pepper*
3–4 *dashes Tabasco sauce*
2 *cloves garlic, pressed*

Clean and devein shrimp and place in a large pan or bowl.

Combine rest of ingredients. Pour over shrimp and marinate several hours, or overnight. Leave in sauce and broil 5 minutes; or, drain and skewer, then charcoal broil 2 to 4 minutes on each side.

*Serves 4 to 6.*


## BEER-BROILED SHRIMP

2 *pounds shrimp*
1 *tablespoon chopped chives*
1 *teaspoon dried basil*
1½ *tablespoons chopped*
   *parsley*

1 *clove garlic, finely*
   *chopped*
½ *teaspoon pepper*
½ *teaspoon celery salt*
¾ *teaspoon salt*
1–1½ *cups beer*

Shell and devein shrimp. Combine rest of ingredients. Marinate shrimp 8 hours or more in refrigerator and stir frequently. Drain thoroughly.

Place shrimps on a hot broiler pan and broil rapidly about 2 minutes on each side.

*Serves 6.*

## FRIED SHRIMP

¾ cup self-rising cornmeal
½ cup self-rising flour
¼ teaspoon salt
1 egg, beaten

¾ cup beer
1 tablespoon vegetable oil
1 pound fresh shrimp,
    peeled and deveined

Blend cornmeal, flour, and salt. Beat egg and beer together and add to flour mixture. Add oil. Mix well.

Coat shrimp on both sides and deep-fry until golden.

*Serves 2 for dinner (4 for a snack).*

## HAWAIIAN SHRIMP

2 pounds raw shrimp,
    shelled and cleaned
1 12-ounce can beer
3 tablespoons cornstarch
¾ cup sugar
¾ cup vinegar
1 green pepper, sliced

Salt to taste
¼ teaspoon monosodium
    glutamate
½ pound almonds, split and
    blanched
1 can pineapple chunks,
    drained

Cook the shrimp in beer until tender but still firm (about 5 minutes). Drain, saving the beer.

Make sweet 'n' sour sauce by mixing the cornstarch and sugar, then adding the vinegar and 1½ cups of beer-shrimp liquid. Cook until clear and thick, stirring constantly. Add cooked shrimp, green pepper, salt, and monosodium glutamate, and cook 3 minutes. Just before serving, stir in nuts and pineapple chunks.

Serve with rice.

*Serves 6.*

## LOBSTER A LA BELGIUM

This is a perfectly elegant dish that is enticingly spiced and might be just the thing for a very special occasion, or an intimate dinner for two.

| | |
|---|---|
| 1 1½–2-pound lobster | 1 tablespoon butter |
| ¼ teaspoon flour | 1½ cups beer |
| 1 tablespoon finely chopped shallots | ¼ teaspoon thyme |
| | 2 egg yolks |
| 1 tablespoon finely chopped carrots | ½ cup heavy cream |
| | ½ cup grated Gruyère |
| 1 tablespoon finely chopped celery | cheese |

Split lobster lengthwise, or have fish market do it. Also have them remove and discard sac and intestine. If there is coral, combine with flour and set aside to add later to sauce with egg yolks. Remove lobster meat and slice it. Reserve lobster shells.

Sauté shallots, carrots, and celery in butter. Add lobster meat and sauté quickly until done. Add beer and thyme; stir. Cover and cook over low heat about 20 minutes. Strain entire mixture. Take liquid only, return it to skillet, and reduce it to ½ cup.

Combine egg yolks blended with cream and the flour/coral mixture (if you have it). Gently add to liquid in skillet and cook sauce until thickened. Don't let it boil. Pour ¼ cup of sauce into the two lobster half-shells and add lobster meat to each, spreading evenly. Cover with remaining sauce. Sprinkle grated cheese over each and brown under broiler. Serve immediately.

*Serves 2.*

## SPANISH MACKEREL STEW

2 *pounds Spanish mackerel,*
  *cleaned and cut into*
  *serving pieces*
Salt to taste
1½ *cups beer*
1 *onion, finely chopped*

1 *bay leaf*
10 *whole peppercorns*
½ *lemon, sliced*
1 *tablespoon butter*
1 *tablespoon flour*
1 *tablespoon sugar*

Sprinkle pieces of fish with salt and let stand 30 minutes. In a stewpot put beer, onion, bay leaf, peppercorns, and lemon; add fish. Over low heat, bring to boil and simmer 20 minutes, or until fish is tender.

Remove fish to a warm platter. Strain liquid. Blend butter with flour and add, with sugar, to strained liquid. Stir constantly until slightly thick, and pour over fish.

*Serves 4 to 6.*

## CODFISH CAKES

2½ *cups flour*
1 *teaspoon baking powder*
1 *clove garlic, finely*
  *chopped*
4 *shallots, finely chopped*
2 *tablespoons chopped*
  *parsley*

¼ *teaspoon black pepper*
1 *cup beer*
1 *pound shredded codfish,*
  *soaked and poached*
Fat for deep frying

Sift flour and baking power together. Add garlic, shallots, parsley, and black pepper. Stir in enough beer to make a batter and add shredded codfish (all the beer may not be necessary).

Heat fat in a deep fryer to 380°. Drop batter by spoonfuls into hot fat and fry until brown. Drain on paper towels.

*Serves 4.*

# Vegetables

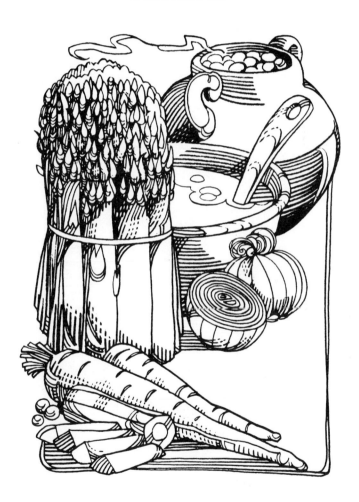

It's always fun to cook vegetables in an elegant or unusual way. Beer, as an added ingredient, is a delightful addition for the adventurous cook. Whether you boil, steam, or fry vegetables, be sure not to overcook. Many partially cooked vegetables may be dipped in batter and deep-fried. So, to begin our chapter, we have a marvelous Beer Batter for Vegetables.

We've included recipes that we've tried ourselves, but we do want to say that you might try substituting beer for water when cooking any vegetable. You'll find it a different and rather pleasant change—even everyday boiled potatoes done in beer! We find this delicious as the potatoes absorb the malt and hop flavor that we enjoy so much. If you try this, do go easy on the salt as beer tends to have a bitterness of its own that usually means less salt!

## BEER BATTER FOR VEGETABLES

Artichokes, asparagus, broccoli, cauliflower, eggplant, okra, and potatoes are delicious fried in this batter!

| | |
|---|---|
| 1¼ *cups all-purpose flour* | 1 *egg, lightly beaten* |
| 1 *teaspoon salt* | 1 *cup beer* |
| 2 *tablespoons shortening* | |

In a mixing bowl, sift together flour and salt. Cut in shortening until mixture resembles fine crumbs.

Add egg and beer and beat until smooth.

*Makes about 2 cups.*

## BEER POTATOES

Here is our favorite recipe utilizing the Beer Batter.

| | |
|---|---|
| 2 *1-pound cans whole* | *Beer Batter for Vegetables* |
| *potatoes* | *(see above)* |
| | *Fat for deep frying* |

Drain potatoes and place on a paper towel to dry. Dip in batter, coating completely. Fry potatoes in deep fat approximately 5 minutes, or until golden. Drain. (If deep fryer is used, have temperature at 365°.)

*Serves 4.*

*Note:* Small, fresh, parboiled potatoes fry up better than the canned variety.

## BEER-BATTER FRITTERS

Here's another batter for frying vegetables. This one is particularly good with zucchini, shrimps, and all those green tomatoes at the end of the summer.

| | |
|---|---|
| 4 *egg yolks* | 1½ *teaspoons salt* |
| 1 *12-ounce can beer* | ½ *teaspoon pepper* |
| 2 *cups sifted flour* | ¼ *cup melted butter* |

Beat together egg yolks and beer. Gradually blend in flour with salt and pepper. Stir in melted butter and let batter rest at room temperature for 1½ hours.

Dust lightly with flour slices of vegetable or green tomatoes. Dip in batter and fry in hot deep fat until golden brown.

*Makes about 3 to 4 cups batter.*

## BEER-BAKED BEANS

After a brisk leaf-raking session on a fall Sunday afternoon, this baked bean dish is a hearty meal in itself. Or, it may be served with leftover cold meats. Except for an occasional peek, it cooks itself.

| | |
|---|---|
| 1 *pound navy beans* | 2 *tablespoons molasses* |
| ½ *pound salt pork, sliced* | 2 *tablespoons catsup* |
| 1½ *teaspoon salt* | 1 *onion, sliced* |
| 2 *tablespoons brown sugar* | 1½ *cups beer* |
| ½ *teaspoon dry mustard* | |

Wash and drain beans, then cover with water and soak overnight.

Drain and place half the beans in a deep oven-proof casserole. Place half of the salt pork over beans. Use half of all ingredients (except beer) and add to salt pork. Then add rest of beans and remaining seasonings.

Top mixture with remaining salt pork. Pour beer over entire mixture. Add more beer, if necessary, to cover beans. Cover and bake at 275° 6 hours. Check every hour to see if liquid is adequate. Add water if necessary.

*Serves 6 to 8.*

## BEER PINTO BEANS

2 *cups dried pinto beans*
¼ *pound salt pork, diced*
1 *teaspoon salt*
⅛ *teaspoon garlic powder*
¼ *teaspoon oregano*

1 *cup chopped fresh tomatoes*
1 *cup chopped green pepper*
1 *cup chopped onion*
2 *tablespoons butter*
1 *cup beer*

Wash and drain beans. In a large, heavy saucepan, cover beans and cook in water to cover, along with salt pork, salt, garlic powder, and oregano. Cook beans until tender, then drain.

Sauté tomatoes, green pepper, and onion in melted butter, stirring often until barely soft. Add beans, mix well, and simmer uncovered 10 minutes. Add beer, stir, and simmer 20 minutes. Serve while hot.

This is great with ham, sausages, and pork.

*Serves 4 to 6.*

## ONIONS AMANDINE

½ *cup sweet butter*
½ *cup blanched shredded almonds*
1 *tablespoon dark brown sugar*

2 *teaspoons chopped garlic*
½ *teaspoon salt*
¼ *teaspoon black pepper*
½ *cup beer*
4 *dozen small white onions*

Melt butter in a heavy casserole and stir in almonds and sugar. Add garlic, seasonings, and beer.

Put in onions and stir until they are well coated. Cover and bake at 350° 1 hour, shaking every 15 minutes. Serve in casserole.

*Serves 6.*

## CARROTS IN BEER

4 *large carrots*                    2 *tablespoons butter*
6 *ounces beer*                      *Salt and pepper to taste*

Peel and cut carrots into long, thin slices. Place in a skillet with beer and butter and cook until tender over low to medium heat about 5 minutes, shaking frequently. Season, and add a little brown sugar if you like them sweet.

*Serves 4.*

## ASPARAGUS A LA PARMESAN

2 *packages frozen asparagus*     ¼ *teaspoon freshly ground*
2 *tablespoons melted butter*        *black pepper*
1 *cup beer*                       ½ *cup grated Parmesan*
½ *teaspoon salt*                    *cheese*

Cook asparagus according to directions on package. Make sure it is not overcooked! Drain.

Place spears in a shallow greased baking dish. Pour melted butter over asparagus and pour beer into baking dish (don't pour beer directly over asparagus). Season with salt and pepper. Sprinkle grated Parmesan cheese on top. Bake at 425° 15 minutes.

When in season, fresh asparagus may be used (2 pounds).

*Serves 6.*

## REGAL CABBAGE

| | |
|---|---|
| 1 *medium head green cabbage* | ½ *cup beer* |
| | ½ *clove garlic, mashed* |
| 1 *14-ounce jar pasteurized processed cheese spread* | 2 *teaspoons Worcestershire sauce* |

Select a solid, round head of cabbage. Remove outer leaves if separated from the stem, and peel off any tough outer leaves. Remove core but leave head of cabbage intact. Place whole head in a deep saucepan and cover with water. Bring to boil and simmer until cabbage leaves are wilted but firm (about 15 minutes). Drain and transfer to a greased 3-quart casserole. Gently open out the leaves but retain the original shape of the cabbage head.

In a small saucepan, heat cheese spread and gradually stir in beer. Add garlic and Worcestershire sauce and stir until smooth. Pour cheese sauce evenly over cabbage; cover casserole. Bake at 350° 40 minutes. Serve hot, cutting into wedges. Spoon cheese sauce over each portion.

*Serves 4 to 6.*

## ZUCCHINI AND PEPPERS

| | |
|---|---|
| 1 *tablespoon cooking oil* | ¼ *teaspoon salt* |
| 1 *clove garlic, minced* | ¼ *teaspoon pepper* |
| 4 *medium zucchini, sliced* | ½ *teaspoon basil* |
| 1 *green pepper, seeded and sliced* | 1 *tablespoon chopped pimiento* |
| 2 *tomatoes, peeled and quartered* | ¾ *cup beer* |

Heat oil in a saucepan and brown garlic lightly. Add zucchini and green pepper and brown lightly. Add remaining ingredients, cover, and simmer about 30 minutes.

*Serves 4.*

## SQUASH ITALIAN STYLE

| | |
|---|---|
| 1 *pound chopped beef* | 1 *teaspoon Italian seasoning* |
| 1 *medium onion, sliced* | 1 *teaspoon salt* |
| *paper-thin* | ¼ *teaspoon garlic powder* |
| 2 *tablespoons olive oil* | 8 *medium green squash* |
| 2 *8-ounce cans tomato sauce* | *(zucchini)* |
| 1 *12-ounce can beer* | 3 *tablespoons Parmesan* |
| 1 *tablespoon sugar* | *cheese* |

In a large skillet, brown chopped beef and onions in olive oil. Add tomato sauce, beer, sugar, and dry seasonings. Simmer gently 40 minutes, stirring occasionally.

Meanwhile wash squash and trim ends. Cook whole in boiling water about 15 minutes, or until fork tender. When cool, cut in half and arrange in one layer in a greased shallow baking dish. Pour meat sauce over squash and sprinkle with cheese. Bake at 350° 45 minutes.

*Serves 8.*

## PRISCILLA JOFFE'S VEGETABLE STEW

This is a rather interesting vegetable dish to serve along with a simple meat course. There are times when a broiled steak or chicken needs perking up, and we found this dish a spicy accompaniment.

| | |
|---|---|
| 3 *large onions* | 3 *large potatoes* |
| 1 *clove garlic* | 1 *teaspoon dried basil* |
| 1 *tablespoon olive oil* | 1 *cup beer* |
| 5 *large green peppers* | 1 *teaspoon salt* |
| 2 *green chili peppers* | ¼ *teaspoon freshly ground* |
| 4 *large tomatoes* | *pepper* |

Cut onions in eighths and mince garlic very fine. Sauté in

oil in medium-sized stewpot until limp and golden brown.

Slice green peppers, chili peppers (*don't forget to discard seeds*), tomatoes, and potatoes, and add to the pot. Pour beer over vegetables, stirring slowly; add seasonings. Stir again and simmer about 45 minutes.

*Serves 4 to 6.*

## RICE STUFFING

This recipe is marvelous for stuffing a fowl, but we found it excellent also as a side dish with chicken or pork.

| | |
|---|---|
| 2 *large green onions, with* | 1 *tablespoon chopped* |
| *tops* | *parsley* |
| 1 *pound chicken gizzards* | 1 *cup water* |
| 1 *pound chicken hearts* | ½ *cup beer* |
| ½ *pound chicken livers* | 2 *cups raw rice, precooked* |
| 1 *large green pepper* | *with 1 teaspoon salt* |
| 4 *stalks celery* | *Salt and pepper to taste* |
| *Oil* | |

Remove onion tops; chop and set aside. In another bowl, chop very fine gizzards, hearts, livers, onions, green pepper, and celery.

Cover bottom of a Dutch oven or heavy saucepan with cooking oil and brown chicken and vegetable mixture. Add chopped parsley and chopped onion tops. Stir in water and beer. Cover and simmer 1 hour.

Add cooked rice and mix. If dry, add small additional amount of beer. Add salt and pepper.

*Stuffs 2 good-sized chickens, or serves 8 to 12 as a side dish.*

## BEEFEATER'S BRUSSELS SPROUTS

Although this is called Beefeater's Brussels Sprouts, we found it was especially good with turkey, duck, or venison.

1 *pound fresh or* 1 *10-ounce*  2 *tablespoons butter*
  *package frozen Brussels*  *Salt and pepper*
  *sprouts*  ¾ *cup seedless white*
*Beer or ale*  *grapes*

Cook Brussels sprouts, using beer for all or part of cooking liquid (if frozen, use all). Drain. Season with butter, salt, and pepper. Add grapes and heat thoroughly.

*Serves 3 to 4.*

## HOLIDAY SWEET POTATOES

3 *large sweet potatoes or*  4 *tablespoons butter*
  *yams*  ½ *cup brown sugar*
6 *slices canned pineapple*  ¾ *cup beer*

Boil sweet potatoes in skins about 20 minutes, or until tender. Peel and halve lengthwise.

Place pineapple slices in a single layer in a shallow baking dish. Top each slice with a potato half, cut side facing down. Melt butter in a small saucepan and add sugar and beer. Stir until sugar is dissolved. Pour mixture over potatoes and pineapple. Bake at 375° 30 minutes, basting often.

*Serves 6.*

## SPRING MELANGE

After a long winter, the appearance of spring brings renewed interest in old favorites. We found this recipe a new twist that is delightful to the palate and the eye, and is a particularly happy accompaniment to roast spring lamb.

2 *tablespoons butter*
3 *tablespoons olive oil*
1 *large onion, finely chopped*
2 *large stalks celery, finely chopped*
1 *pound yellow crookneck squash, diced*
1 *pound zucchini, thinly sliced*

1 *pound summer squash, thinly sliced*
¾ *cup beer (or bock beer)*
¼ *teaspoon crumbled basil*
1 *teaspoon salt*
¼ *teaspoon pepper*
¼ *teaspoon tarragon*

Melt butter and oil together in a large saucepan. Sauté onion, celery, and squashes until celery is tender and onion clear. Add beer and seasonings. Cover and simmer about 20 minutes, or until tender.

*Serves 8 to 10.*

# Salads and
# Salad Dressings

**A**lthough tossed green salads are always welcome, put a little more fun in the salad department by experimenting with something different. We've included a variety of formulas, beginning with the often forgotten German Potato Salad. If you'll treat this natural gem with the respect it deserves, the rewards will be delightful eating! We believe the dressings are superb. Use your imagination; try the Creamy Salad Dressing with a cucumber and carrot salad, or marinated artichoke hearts. Innovate, create! The challenge is: How great a salad can you serve without using lettuce?

## GERMAN POTATO SALAD

4 *pounds potatoes*
6 *slices bacon*
1 *cup diced celery*
2 *tablespoons chopped
    onion*
4 *teaspoons salt*
½ *cup butter*

¼ *cup flour*
½ *teaspoon dry mustard*
3 *tablespoons sugar*
1 *cup beer*
1 *teaspoon Tabasco sauce*
3 *tablespoons chopped
    parsley*

Cook potatoes in skins until barely tender. Peel and dice into a 3-quart casserole. While potatoes are cooking, fry and drain bacon. Crumble, mix with chopped celery, onion, and 2 teaspoons salt; set aside.

In a saucepan melt butter, then add flour, mustard, sugar, and remaining 2 teaspoons salt. Stir until smooth. Gradually add beer and Tabasco sauce. Stir over medium heat until mixture thickens and comes to boil. Pour over potatoes and sprinkle with parsley. Mix lightly and let stand 1 hour. Add bacon mixture, and blend gently.

If necessary, you may cover and reheat in oven at 375° 5 minutes, or until warm.

*Serves 10 to 12.*

## COLE SLAW

6 *cups shredded cabbage*
1 *green pepper, diced*
½ *cup beer*
1 *cup mayonnaise*

1 *teaspoon salt*
¼ *teaspoon dry mustard*
2 *teaspoons minced onion*
1 *teaspoon celery seed*

Mix cabbage and green pepper and set aside. Blend beer into mayonnaise and add remaining ingredients. Pour beer-mayonnaise mixture over cabbage, mix well, and refrigerate for at least 1 hour before serving.

*Serves 8.*

## LENTIL SALAD

A superb accompaniment to roast lamb or pork, we also found this an unusual side dish at an outdoor buffet.

2 *cups dried lentils*
1 *quart water*
1 *pint beer*
2 *bay leaves*
1 *large onion, pierced with 8 cloves*
1½ *teaspoons salt*
4 *tablespoons salad oil*
3 *tablespoons cider vinegar*
¼ *teaspoon pepper*
½ *teaspoon dry mustard*
½ *teaspoon paprika*
6 *scallions, sliced*
6 *scallion tops, finely chopped*
½ *cup chopped dill pickles*
2 *cups shredded cabbage*
5 *medium potatoes, boiled and thinly sliced*
2 *tablespoons minced parsley*

Rinse lentils and place in a large pot with water, beer, bay leaves, and onion. Add 1 teaspoon salt. Cover and bring to boil. Lower heat and simmer 45 minutes.

Remove onion and bay leaves, and drain. Combine oil, vinegar, rest of salt, pepper, mustard, paprika, sliced scallions, scallion tops, and pickles, and mix well for dressing. Arrange shredded cabbage on a small platter and place potato slices on top. Then place drained lentils in individual mounds to serve 6, and pour dressing over entire platter.

Sprinkle with parsley and chill before serving.

*Serves 6.*

## CAESAR SALAD

| | |
|---|---|
| 2 *tablespoons butter* | 4 *tablespoons lemon juice* |
| 4 *slices bread, thinly sliced* | ⅓ *cup beer* |
| 2 *cloves garlic* | 8 *tablespoons grated* |
| *Salt* | *Parmesan cheese* |
| 4 *small heads romaine* | 12 *anchovy fillets* |
| *lettuce (or 2 large)* | 1 *1-minute coddled egg* |
| 8 *tablespoons olive oil* | |

Make croutons by buttering bread on both sides, cubing it small, and browning in oven. Rub a salad bowl with garlic and sprinkle bowl with salt. Tear lettuce into bite-sizes. Sprinkle with croutons. Mix oil, lemon juice, beer, and cheese, then add mashed anchovy fillets. Add egg to dressing and work smooth. Pour over lettuce and croutons. Toss well.

*Serves 8.*

## JELLO SALAD

Here's a gelatin salad that isn't too delicate for a man's appetite or taste. Full-flavored and tart, it goes very well with beef or pork.

| | |
|---|---|
| 2 *packages unflavored* | ½ *cup finely chopped green* |
| *gelatin* | *onions or chives* |
| 2 *cups hot water* | ½ *cup finely chopped* |
| 2 *cups beer* | *cucumber, drained* |
| 1½ *tablespoons horseradish* | |

Dissolve gelatin in hot water; cool, and refrigerate. When gelatin is beginning to jell, add beer and horseradish and beat well. Return to refrigerator. When gelatin is half con-

gealed, add onions and chopped cucumber. Return to refrigerator until firm.

*Serves 6.*

## CREAMY SALAD DRESSING

½ *cup chopped onion*          ¼ *cup beer*
1 *clove garlic*              ½ *cup chili sauce*
2 *tablespoons butter*        *Juice of* ½ *lemon*
¾ *cup sour cream*

Sauté onion and garlic in butter. Discard garlic and let
onions cool. In a small bowl, mix sour cream, beer, chili
sauce, lemon juice, and onions. Stir well and chill thoroughly. Pour over salad greens.

*Makes 2 cups.*

## BEER DRESSING

This one is great over potatoes for a really different potato
salad, or over fish salad. It also goes well with sliced tomatoes and celery.

1 *cup French dressing*       1 *teaspoon chives*
   (*your own or bottled*)    1 *teaspoon chopped green*
⅓ *cup beer*                     *pepper*
1 *teaspoon grated onion*     ½ *cup green celery leaves*
1 *teaspoon chopped parsley*

Add all other ingredients to French dressing and blend well.

*Makes about 1½ cups.*

# Cheese Dishes

To all those in search of real culinary adventures, the most varied fare is surely reflected in cheese dishes and fondues. Your cooking will flourish and you'll earn a reputation as a gourmet cook when you serve the unusual recipes that follow. They're all simple and inspiring. Fondues and rarebits are always welcome at Sunday brunch, as an appetizer, for a late evening snack, or for that special moment when you want something different. Use your chafing dishes or fondue pots. If you have none, any flameproof casserole over a candle-warmer or Sterno can will do just as well.

Fondues are high fashion and if you serve one as the main course, you might consider starting dinner with one of the more elaborate hors d'oeuvres like Deviled Clams or Party Shrimp Pie. These combine protein with economy, and they are elegant.

## CHEESE FONDUE

½ pound Cheddar cheese          ¼ teaspoon pepper
½ pound Gruyère cheese          1 clove garlic
½ tablespoon cornstarch         1½ cups beer
½ teaspoon salt                 Dash Tabasco sauce

Grate both Cheddar and Gruyère cheese into a bowl. Combine cheeses with cornstarch and salt and pepper.

Rub garlic clove over inside of a fondue pan (or heavy chafing dish that can be placed over an alcohol flame). Pour in beer and heat slowly on top of stove. Gradually add cheese mixture and stir constantly until melted. Stir until creamy. Add Tabasco sauce.

Serve in fondue pot over alcohol flame to keep hot. If necessary, thin with more beer. Serve with crusty cubes of Italian or French bread, for dipping.

*Serves 8 as an appetizer, otherwise serves 4.*

## CHEESE RAREBIT

1½ tablespoons butter           ½ teaspoon salt
1½ tablespoons flour            ½ teaspoon chili powder
1½ cups beer                    Pinch cayenne pepper
1 cup grated American
  cheese

Melt butter, add flour, and blend well. Slowly add beer and stir over low flame until slightly thick. Add cheese and continue to stir until melted and well blended. Add seasonings.

Serve over hot buttered toast.

*Serves 4.*

## JANE DONNELLY'S WELSH RAREBIT

1 *teaspoon Worcestershire*    ½ *cup beer*
  *sauce*                                1 *cup shredded sharp*
½ *teaspoon dry mustard*     *Cheddar cheese*
*Dash paprika*

Combine Worcestershire sauce, mustard, and paprika in a saucepan. Add beer and let stand over low heat until beer heats through. Stir in cheese and continue to stir until cheese has melted. *Do not overheat!*

Serve over toast on heated plates.

*Serves 4.*

## SHRIMP RAREBIT

1 *pound Cheddar cheese,*    1 *cup shrimp, cooked and*
  *diced*                               *diced*
1 *tablespoon butter*        ¼ *cup finely chopped green*
½ *teaspoon salt*              *pepper*
½ *teaspoon paprika*      1 *tablespoon finely chopped*
1 *teaspoon dry mustard*     *onion*
1 *cup beer*

In top of a double boiler melt cheese and butter. Then add seasonings and beer, stirring constantly. When cheese mixture is smooth add shrimp, green pepper, and onion. Continue stirring until heated through. If too thick, thin with beer.

Serve over toast.

*Serves 6.*

## BEER RAREBIT

2 teaspoons Worcestershire sauce
½ teaspoon dry mustard
Dash cayenne pepper or Tabasco sauce

¼ teaspoon paprika
½ cup beer
1 pound shredded sharp Cheddar cheese

In top of a double boiler, mix Worcestershire sauce, mustard, pepper or Tabasco sauce, and paprika. Add beer and cook until beer is heated. Add cheese, stirring until it has melted.

Serve on toast cut into triangles.

*Serves 6.*

## RAREBIT WITH SAUSAGES

1½ pounds Cheddar cheese, grated
3 tablespoons butter
1 12-ounce can beer

4 egg yolks
1 pound "brown-and-serve" sausages
½ cup beer

Melt cheese and butter in top of a double boiler. Add ½ can beer and stir until smooth. Beat egg yolks, add remaining ½ can beer and blend with cheese. Cook slowly, stirring constantly, until thick.

Brown sausages and add ½ cup beer. Cover and simmer until beer has evaporated.

Serve rarebit over warm toast and top with sausages.

*Serves 4.*

## RAREBIT WITH OYSTERS

| | |
|---|---|
| 2 *tablespoons butter* | 1½ *teaspoons dry mustard* |
| 3 *cups grated Cheddar* | 1 *teaspoon salt* |
| *cheese* | ¾ *teaspoon paprika* |
| 1 *cup beer* | 1 *cup small oysters, drained* |

Melt butter and cheese in top of a double boiler. Slowly add beer (reserving 1½ tablespoons), and stir until smooth. Blend seasonings with 1½ tablespoons beer and stir into cheese mixture.

Add oysters and cook rarebit a few minutes until piping hot.

Serve over toast triangles.

*Serves 4.*

## ONION 'N' CHEESE RAREBIT

| | |
|---|---|
| 1 *cup beer* | ½ *teaspoon Worcestershire* |
| 2 *cups grated American* | *sauce* |
| *cheese* | 1 *egg, beaten* |
| 1 *tablespoon butter* | 6 *slices toast* |
| ½ *teaspoon salt* | 1 *3½-ounce can* |
| *Dash black pepper* | *French-fried onions* |
| ½ *teaspoon dry mustard* | |

Combine beer, cheese, butter, and seasonings in top of a double boiler. Cook over hot water until cheese is melted, stirring constantly. Gradually stir in egg and cook until thickened, stirring constantly.

Serve on toast and top with warmed onions.

*Serves 6.*

## WISCONSIN RAREBIT

2 *tablespoons butter*
1 *pound (4 cups) grated*
  *Cheddar cheese*
¾ *cup beer*
½ *teaspoon salt*

1 *teaspoon dry mustard*
*Dash cayenne pepper*
1 *teaspoon Worcestershire*
  *sauce*
1 *egg yolk*

In top of a double boiler melt butter; add cheese, stirring occasionally until melted. Add beer, salt, mustard, pepper, and Worcestershire sauce, and stir until smooth.

Beat egg yolk in a small bowl. Gradually add a little of the cheese-beer mixture, stirring constantly to prevent curdling. Pour back into cheese-beer mixture. Stir until thickened, but do not boil.

Serve on buttered toast.

*Serves 4.*

# Eggs

**E**ggs are one of the basic and simple foods, but they're surely the most versatile. There is no need to be bored with an egg simply because you are tired of the usual fried, poached, and scrambled.

The egg recipes contained in this chapter are delicious. Try all of them, and perhaps you will be inspired to create some of your own.

Eggs should always be fresh, and remember to remove them from the refrigerator about one-half hour before using. The Beer Omelet, especially, needs eggs at room temperature. This recipe is for one serving and if you're going to serve more than one, we suggest you prepare each individually.

All of these recipes can be served at any time of day; that is the magic of eggs. What is perfect for breakfast is also a cook's delight for a simple lunch or supper.

## BEER OMELET FOR ONE

| | |
|---|---|
| 1 *slice bread, stale* | 2 *tablespoons butter* |
| ¼ *cup beer* | ¼ *cup diced Gruyère* |
| 3 *eggs* | *cheese* |

Cut bread into small pieces and soak in beer until softened. Beat eggs and blend bread mixture into eggs, stirring very well.

Melt butter in a 7-inch skillet, pour in egg mixture, and add cheese. Cook over low heat until set. Brown top lightly under broiler.

*Serves 1.*

## CREAMY SCRAMBLED EGGS

This is a superb luncheon or brunch dish.

| | |
|---|---|
| 1 *3-ounce package cream cheese* | 6 *eggs* |
| 3 *tablespoons melted butter* | 2 *tablespoons butter* |
| ⅓ *cup beer* | ½ *medium onion, minced very fine* |
| ¼ *cup chopped olives* | 1 *tablespoon parsley* |
| ¼ *teaspoon salt* | |

Have cream cheese at room temperature. Then place in a mixing bowl with melted butter, and mix well. Blend in beer, olives, and salt.

Beat eggs lightly with a wire whisk and add to cheese mixture. Melt 2 tablespoons butter in a skillet and sauté onion and parsley until onion is limp. Then add egg-cheese mixture and cook over low heat, stirring constantly until eggs are scrambled.

*Serves 4.*

## BAKED EGGS

¾ *stick butter*　　　　　2 *cups cracker crumbs*
1 *cup chopped onions*　　1 *cup grated cheese*
1 *cup chopped green pepper*　¾ *cup beer*
8 *eggs*

Melt butter, add onions and green peppers. Sauté 15 minutes over a low flame. Pour into bottom of an oblong baking dish.

Break open eggs and place one at a time over the cooked onions and peppers. Cover with crumbs and grated cheese. Pour beer over this. Bake at 325° 20 to 30 minutes.

*Serves 4.*

## POACHED EGGS WITH HORSERADISH SAUCE

8 *eggs*　　　　　　　⅓ *cup beer*
4 *English muffins*　　　2½ *tablespoons horseradish*
¼ *teaspoon salt and pepper*　1 *teaspoon crumbled bacon*
1 *cup sour cream*　　　½ *teaspoon chopped chives*

Poach eggs in salted water until set. Toast English muffins and place a poached egg on each half. Season with salt and pepper. Place on a cookie sheet.

Blend sour cream, beer, and horseradish until smooth. Pour sauce over each egg, covering muffin sides as well. Sprinkle with bacon bits and chopped chives and place under broiler 1 minute, or until bubbling.

*Serves 4.*

# Breads

In these hectic days of the twentieth century, nothing is more satisfying than an occasional reunion with the past. The delicious aroma of homemade bread is most rewarding and a welcome return to old-fashioned home-making. You'll find the following bread recipes fairly simple. Some take longer than others, but they're all well worth it, and you'll find the addition of beer an agreeable seasoning. The herbs in the beer enhance the yeast-like flavor, and you'll be pleasantly surprised at its mellowness.

*Note:* As we stated earlier in the book, beer should always be at room temperature for use in cooking. This is particularly important to remember in the bread and cake recipes which follow in the next two chapters.

## BEER AND MALT BREAD

| | |
|---|---|
| 1 *envelope yeast* | 1 *tablespoon salt* |
| ¼ *cup lukewarm water* | 4 *cups sifted unbleached* |
| 1 *12-ounce can beer* | *flour* |
| 1 *tablespoon powdered* | ¼ *cup cornmeal* |
| *bakers' malt or malt syrup* | 1 *egg white, unbeaten* |
| 1 *tablespoon butter* | *Poppy or sesame seeds* |
| 1 *tablespoon sugar* | |

Dissolve yeast in water. Heat beer to a gentle simmer, then remove from heat and add malt, butter, sugar, and salt. Stir until completely dissolved. Put mixture into a large bowl; cool until lukewarm, and stir in yeast mixture. Add 2 cups flour and beat the dough until smooth. Slowly add remaining 2 cups flour and work the dough until it forms a ball and leaves the sides of the bowl.

Place dough on a floured board or pastry cloth, then strike the dough smartly with the edge of your floured hand and fold it in half as it flattens. Continue this process approximately 2 minutes. Knead dough about 5 minutes until smooth and elastic, then place it in a buttered bowl and butter top of it.

Cover dough with a towel and place in a warm spot for approximately 1 hour, or until size doubles. Punch the dough down and knead it on a floured board about 2 minutes, then cut it in half and let the two pieces rest 10 minutes.

Shape each piece into a narrow rectangle by folding the long sides to the center and pinching the seams together. Oil a baking sheet and sprinkle generously with cornmeal. Place loaves on baking sheet seam side down, cover with towel, and put in a warm place to rise until size has almost doubled. Then brush tops with egg white and sprinkle with poppy or sesame seeds. Preheat oven to 375° and place pan of boiling water on bottom of oven. Slash tops of loaves ¼ inch deep in several spots. Bake bread at 375° 20 minutes, then reduce heat to 350° for an additional 15 minutes until well browned.

Cool loaves on racks.

## BEER-CHEESE BREAD

This easy-to-store, attractive bread is a favorite of Mrs. Edward Berman, who created this recipe, and her family. They keep it on hand to serve to their many relatives and numerous friends when they drop in for a quick visit.

2 cups beer
1 15-ounce box raisins
5 cups all-purpose flour
1¼ cups sugar
1 tablespoon baking soda
1½ teaspoons nutmeg
½ teaspoon salt
3 eggs, well beaten
2½ cups grated American cheese
2 cups chopped walnuts

Preheat oven to 350°. Heat beer to boiling point and pour over raisins. Let stand in bowl while you mix other ingredients. Combine flour, sugar, baking soda, nutmeg, and salt. Stir in eggs, beer and raisins, cheese, and walnuts. Mix thoroughly. Pour into well-greased 9″ x 5″ loaf pans. Bake 45 minutes, or until a toothpick inserted in the center comes out clean.

This tasty loaf may be served warm or cold and is delicious with butter, marmalade, or cream cheese.

*Note:* This recipe may also be made in muffin pans. Bake at 350° 35 minutes. Yields 4 dozen.

## BEER 'N' RYE BREAD

4 *cups beer*
1 *cup maple syrup*
6 *cakes yeast*
9 *cups rye flour*

9 *cups white flour*
2 *teaspoons salt*
¾ *cup orange peel slivers,*
    *membranes removed*

Heat beer and syrup together until lukewarm. Pour mixture over yeast and stir until dissolved. In a bowl combine rye flour, white flour, salt, and orange peel slivers. Add beer-yeast mixture and make a smooth dough by thoroughly mixing all ingredients. Stand in a warm place about ¾ hour, or until dough has doubled in volume.

Knead dough, form into 3 long loaves, and place in greased, floured bread tins. Sprinkle with flour, cover, and let stand until almost doubled. Preheat oven to 400°. Bake 15 minutes, then reduce heat to 325° for 15 more minutes, then to 300° for final 30 minutes.

## BUSY DAY BREAD

1 *12-ounce can beer*
4 *tablespoons margarine*
2 *13¾-ounce packages hot*
    *roll mix*

2 *eggs*
5 *tablespoons sugar*
1 *cup wheat germ*

Heat beer and margarine until beer is warm. Add yeast from the two packages of roll mix and dissolve.

Beat eggs. Add sugar, eggs, wheat germ, and remainder of roll mix and mix thoroughly. Place contents in a greased pan and let rise in a warm place until dough has doubled in volume.

Knead down and shape into 2 loaves. Place into greased loaf

pans and allow dough to rise again until doubled in size. Bake at 350° 40 to 45 minutes.

## BEER HUSH PUPPIES

When hunters' dogs would whine and beg for the good-smelling food around the campfires, the men tossed left-over corn patties to them calling, "Hush puppies." This was enough to still their hunger and quiet them.

| | |
|---|---|
| 2 *cups self-rising cornmeal* | 1 *egg, beaten* |
| 1 *tablespoon sugar* | ¾ *cup beer* |
| 1 *small onion, finely chopped* | |

Mix cornmeal and sugar together. Add onion, egg, and beer. Lightly stir.

Drop by teaspoonfuls into hot deep fat (360°). Fry a few at a time to keep fat at same temperature. Fry until golden brown, then drain on absorbent paper. Serve hot.

*Makes 2 dozen.*

## QUICKIE PUPPIES

| | |
|---|---|
| 1 *cup pancake mix* | 2 *tablespoons chopped green pepper* |
| 1 *cup cornmeal* | |
| 1 *teaspoon baking powder* | 3 *slices bacon, cooked and crumbled* |
| ½ *teaspoon salt* | |
| 2 *tablespoons chopped onion* | About ½ *cup beer* |
| | *Cooking oil* |

Mix all ingredients together. Use enough beer to make batter proper consistency to drop from teaspoon into hot cooking oil. Fry until brown, then drain on paper towels; serve immediately.

*Makes 2 dozen.*

## ONION HERB BREAD

1 13¾-ounce package hot roll mix
¾ cup beer
2 eggs
1¼ teaspoons onion salt
1 teaspoon Italian seasoning
1 3½-ounce can French-fried onions

Sprinkle yeast from roll mix over beer and stir to dissolve. Blend in eggs. Add onion salt, Italian seasoning, onions, and dry roll mix. Beat about 2 minutes, by hand.

Pour into a greased 2-quart casserole. Cover and let rise in a warm place until doubled in size. Bake at 375° 30 minutes, or until a deep golden brown. Remove from pan immediately.

*Note:* This can also be baked in a loaf pan.

## DEVILED CORNBREAD

1 10-ounce package cornbread mix
1 2¼-ounce can deviled ham
1 egg
½ cup beer
1 teaspoon sesame seeds (optional)

Combine cornbread mix, ham, egg, and beer. Blend well. Pour into a greased 8-inch-square pan. Sprinkle top with sesame seeds if desired.

Follow package directions for oven temperature and baking time. Serve warm.

*Serves 6.*

Breads

## CREAMY SPRING SQUARES

¾ cup sour cream
1 ¼-ounce package onion
  dip mix

1 egg, slightly beaten
3 cups biscuit mix
1 cup beer

Blend sour cream, onion dip mix, and egg; set aside. Combine biscuit mix and beer; stir until dough forms. Lightly pat into a well-greased 9-inch-square baking pan. Spread onion mixture over top. Bake at 450° 20 minutes.

Cut into squares and serve hot.

*Makes 9 squares.*

## LIMPA

1 12-ounce can beer
2 tablespoons fennel seeds
1 tablespoon white vinegar
¼ cup molasses
¼ cup dark corn syrup
2 teaspoons salt

2 packages granular yeast
2 tablespoons softened
  butter
4 cups finely sifted rye flour
1¾–2 cups sifted white
  flour

Heat beer until lukewarm. Combine in a large bowl with fennel seeds, vinegar, molasses, corn syrup, and salt. Sprinkle yeast into this mixture and stir until dissolved. Beat in butter. Stir in rye flour and 1½ cups white flour. Mix well.

Turn dough onto a baking board (sprinkling baking board with remaining flour) and knead with floured hands until smooth and elastic. Make sure dough is no longer sticky.

Place dough in a greased bowl and turn to grease all sides. Cover and let rise in a warm place until doubled in size (about 2 hours).

Punch down, pull edges toward center, and turn dough in

bowl. Let rise again until almost doubled (about 45 minutes).

Turn dough out onto floured board and divide into 2 portions. Knead for 2 minutes and shape each piece into a round loaf. Place on a buttered cookie sheet and let rise again until doubled (about 50 minutes). Bake at 350° 35 to 40 minutes.

## ITALIAN POPOVERS

1 6-ounce package popover
  mix
⅓ cup grated Parmesan
  cheese

2 eggs
1¼ cups beer

Combine all ingredients in a bowl. Beat with an electric mixer until smooth (about 3 minutes). (Batter will be thin.)

Pour into six 5-ounce well-greased custard cups, filling each about two-thirds full. Place cups on a baking sheet. Bake at 450° 20 minutes. Reduce temperature to 350° and bake 30 minutes more. Let stand several minutes; loosen popovers around the edges and remove from cups. Serve with hot butter.

*Makes 6.*

# Desserts

If by now you're a confirmed lover of beer cookery, you'll understand that it certainly has a rightful place in this chapter. The taste when drinking beer and ales is *not* the same as when cooking with beer and ales. As you know, the low alcohol content immediately cooks away and what remains are the herbs, hops, and grain flavors that are so right for cakes and cookies. Whether you prefer Apple Fritters, Hawaiian Cookies, or any other recipe in this section, you'll find they're all a memorable finale to any meal.

## GLORIA SPATER'S APPLE FRITTERS

Sweet and delicious as a dessert should be, apples are a great treat any season or served with any course. Gloria Spater's Apple Fritters are a grand accompaniment to roast chicken, or our Spicy Pork Chops. This recipe can be served as a dessert or with meat. Other fruits may be substituted —pears or peaches are especially good.

| | |
|---|---|
| 6 *apples, peeled and cored* | 2 *tablespoons vegetable oil* |
| *Juice of 1 lemon* | *or melted butter* |
| 1 *cup flour* | *Pinch salt* |
| 2 *eggs, separated* | *Sugar* |
| ¾ *cup beer* | *Vegetable oil for deep-fat frying* |

Slice apples into rings about ¾ inch thick. Drop into plastic bag with lemon juice to keep from discoloring. Turn over so slices are well coated with the juice.

Combine flour, egg yolks, beer, oil or butter, salt, and pinch of sugar in a bowl. Beat until smooth. Beat egg whites until firm and carefully fold into flour mixture just before using. Pour enough oil in a deep pan to deep-fry. Heat until it reaches 350° on a candy thermometer, or until a cube of bread browns in 60 seconds.

To fry fritters, dip apple rings into batter, shake off any excess, then drop into hot oil. Fry until golden on both sides. Drain. Sprinkle lightly with granulated sugar.

When all the fritters are cooked and drained, place them on a cookie sheet and put under broiler just long enough to melt sugar and glaze fritters. Don't leave them! It takes just seconds.

*Serves 6.*

Note: When used as a dessert, we recommend topping with whipped cream or ice cream.

# Desserts

## HAWAIIAN COOKIES

1 *pound shortening or*    2 *tablespoons flour*
   *butter*                  2 *#303 cans crushed*
2 *pounds flour, sifted*       *pineapple*
6 *ounces beer*                ¼ *cup cinnamon*
1¼ *cups sugar*

Cut shortening or butter into flour and sprinkle slowly with beer until dough is smooth and can be rolled out. Meanwhile, add 1 cup sugar and 2 tablespoons flour to pineapple and heat in a saucepan until thick. Cool.

Roll out dough ⅛ inch thick. Using a circle or cookie cutter, cut 3-inch circles. Place filling on half of circle and fold over. Seal edges. Pierce top with fork.

Bake at 425° on an ungreased cookie sheet ½ inch apart 12 minutes. While warm, sprinkle with a mixture of cinnamon and remaining sugar.

*Makes 5 dozen cookies.*

## APRICOT COOKIES

4 *cups sifted flour*      12 *ounces commercial*
½ *pound margarine*        *apricot filling or apricot*
¾ *cup beer*               *preserves*
                      ¼ *cup cinnamon*
                      ¼ *cup sugar*

Pour flour into a large bowl and cut in margarine with a pastry blender or two knives. Gradually add beer slowly, mixing constantly, until dough is consistency for rolling. Roll out dough very thin, about ⅛ inch thick. Cut out 3-inch rounds with a cookie cutter and spoon ½ teaspoon of apricot filling on half of cookie dough; fold over, sealing edges tightly. Pierce tops 3 or 4 times with a toothpick.

Place on an ungreased cookie sheet about 1 inch apart and bake at 425° 10 to 12 minutes, or until golden brown.

While cookies are baking, mix cinnamon and sugar together and set aside. When cookies are done and still hot, sprinkle with cinnamon-sugar mixture; set aside on racks to cool.

*Makes about 6 dozen.*


## HOLIDAY BEER CAKE

A moist and fruity cake with a surprise in every bite!

| | |
|---|---|
| 2⅔ cups cake flour | ½ cup margarine or butter |
| ½ teaspoon salt | 1 cup molasses |
| 1 tablespoon baking powder | 1½ cups beer |
| ¼ teaspoon baking soda | ¾ cup chopped dates |
| ½ teaspoon cinnamon | ¾ cup coarsely chopped |
| ¼ teaspoon ginger | nuts |
| ½ teaspoon nutmeg | |

Preheat oven to 350°. Grease a 9-inch angel-food cake pan and dust with a light coat of flour.

Sift together cake flour, salt, baking powder, baking soda, cinnamon, ginger, and nutmeg. Heat margarine, molasses, and beer in a pan, stirring gently until margarine melts.

Stir in dates and allow mixture to cool 15 minutes. Mix sifted ingredients with beer mixture until well blended. Add nuts. Bake 1 hour, or until cake springs back when gently pressed with a finger.

This cake remains fresh and moist until the last yummy crumb has vanished.

## COZY KITCHEN CAKE

| | |
|---|---|
| 1½ cups brown sugar | 1½ teaspoons cinnamon |
| 1 teaspoon salt | 1½ teaspoons allspice |
| ¾ cup margarine | 1 teaspoon powdered cloves |
| 2 eggs | ½ teaspoon baking soda |
| 2¼ cups flour | 2 cups beer |
| 1½ teaspoons baking powder | |

Cream sugar, salt, and margarine. Add eggs and mix well. In a separate bowl blend flour, baking powder, spices, and baking soda. Slowly combine dry ingredients with creamed mixture. Add beer gradually as you go along. Beat thoroughly until smooth. Pour into two greased 8-inch cake pans and bake at 375° 35 minutes.

Frost with your favorite vanilla icing.

## BUSY DAY DEVIL'S FOOD CAKE

| | |
|---|---|
| 2 squares bitter chocolate | ½ teaspoon salt |
| ½ cup boiling water | ⅓ cup margarine |
| ¾ teaspoon baking soda | 1 cup sugar |
| 1½ cups cake flour | 2 eggs |
| 1½ teaspoons baking powder | ½ cup beer |
| | 1 teaspoon vanilla |

Preheat oven to 375°. Grease two 8-inch layer pans or one 7" x 11" oblong pan. Line bottom of pan with wax paper. Combine chocolate and boiling water in top of a double boiler. Stir until melted. Stir in baking soda and set aside to cool.

Combine flour, baking powder, and salt. In another bowl,

cream margarine and sugar until light and fluffy. Lightly beat eggs and add to sugar mixture. Alternately add flour mixture and beer, a little of each at a time. Add cooled chocolate mixture and vanilla, gently folding in until well blended.

Bake 30 to 35 minutes, or until cake shrinks from sides of pan. Cool and frost with your favorite frosting.

## COFFEE CAKE

A great cake for cake sales and thank-you gifts.

½ cup warm beer
1 package dry yeast
½ cup flour
1 egg
Juice of 1 lemon
⅛ teaspoon nutmeg

¼ cup sugar
½ teaspoon salt
3 tablespoons margarine
¾ cup beer
3½ cups sifted flour

Pour warm beer over yeast and ½ cup flour. Allow to stand 10 minutes.

Beat yeast mixture, egg, lemon juice, nutmeg, sugar, salt, margarine, ¾ cup beer, and 3 cups sifted flour until mixture forms a medium-soft dough. Use the remaining ½ cup flour to flour table or pastry cloth. Work dough, kneading until soft and easy to handle.

Place in a greased bowl; cover until doubled in size (1 to 1½ hours). Knead lightly. Place in greased shallow pan, brush with melted margarine, and let rise again until doubled in size. Top with Streusel Topping (see page 143) and bake at 350° until light brown (approximately 45 minutes).

142

# Desserts

## Streusel Topping

2¼ *sticks margarine*  1 *egg*
2 *cups sugar*  ¼ *cup sugar*
3 *cups flour*  1 *teaspoon vanilla*
1 *teaspoon cinnamon*  ½ *cup chopped walnuts*

Using a pie blender or two knives, cut margarine, 2 cups sugar, and flour to the consistency of coarse crumbs. Add cinnamon and set aside. In a small bowl, beat egg, ¼ cup sugar, and vanilla, and spread on top of raised dough of coffee cake. Sprinkle with chopped nuts. Top with the coarse crumb mixture and bake.

## JIFFY CHOCOLATE CAKE #1

Busy day—company coming? Here's a winner.

1 *package chocolate cake*  1⅓ *cups beer*
*mix*  2 *eggs*

Preheat oven to 350°. Grease and flour two 8-inch cake pans or one 9″ x 13″ oblong pan. Blend ingredients well and then beat at medium speed 4 minutes.

Pour batter into prepared pans and bake 30 to 35 minutes. Cake is done if it springs back when gently pressed with a finger. Frost with Chocolate Beer Icing (page 147).

## JIFFY CHOCOLATE CAKE #2

1 *package fudge cake mix*  ⅓ *cup cooking oil*
1 *package instant chocolate*  3 *eggs*
*pudding mix*  1 *cup beer*

Place all ingredients in a large mixing bowl. Blend until well moistened. Beat at medium speed 10 minutes. Pour into 10-inch greased pan, or tube pan. Bake at 350° 1 hour.

143

## BREWER'S BEST FRUITCAKE

¾ cup butter
3 cups sifted flour
2 teaspoons baking powder
1 teaspoon salt
2 teaspoons cinnamon
½ teaspoon allspice
½ teaspoon cloves
½ teaspoon nutmeg
1 pound (or 2½ cups) mixed
    candied fruit
½ cup candied pineapple
½ pound (or 1¼ cups)
    whole candied cherries

1 pound (or 3 cups) raisins
1¼ cups dates, cut in large
    pieces
2 cups coarsely chopped
    nuts
4 eggs
1¾ cups firmly packed
    brown sugar
1 cup beer
¼ cup molasses

Melt butter, cool, and set aside. Sift together in a large bowl flour, baking powder, salt, cinnamon, allspice, cloves, and nutmeg. Add mixed candied fruit, pineapple, cherries, raisins, dates, and nuts. Mix to coat fruit with dry ingredients.

Beat eggs until foamy and gradually add brown sugar, beating until well combined. Blend in beer, molasses, and the cooled butter. Add to flour-fruit mixture and stir until well combined.

Grease well one 10-inch tube pan, two 9″ x 3″ pans, four 1-pound coffee cans, or six #2 cans. Line with wax paper. Turn batter into pans, filling ⅔ to ¾ full.

Bake at 275° 2½ to 3 hours. Cool thoroughly before removing from pans.

*Note:* To remove cakes from #2 cans, cut out bottom of can and loosen cake from sides with a spatula.

## OLD-FASHIONED NUTMEG CAKE

Folks young and old love this cake.

| | |
|---|---|
| ½ *cup margarine* | 1 *teaspoon baking powder* |
| 1½ *cups sugar* | ½ *teaspoon salt* |
| 3 *eggs, lightly beaten* | 2 *teaspoons nutmeg* |
| 2 *cups sifted cake flour* | 1 *cup beer* |
| ¾ *teaspoon baking soda* | 1 *teaspoon vanilla* |

Preheat oven to 400°. Grease and flour an 11″ x 7″ pan, or sheet pan, if thinner pieces are desired. Cream margarine and sugar. Add eggs and beat thoroughly.

Sift together all dry ingredients. Add dry ingredients to creamed mixture alternately with beer. Add vanilla. Pour into prepared pan and bake 20 minutes, or until done.

Spread with Broiled Frosting (see page 146) and cut in squares.

## MELT-IN-YOUR-MOUTH SPICE CAKE

| | |
|---|---|
| ½ *cup margarine or other* | ½ *teaspoon baking soda* |
|   *shortening* | ¼ *teaspoon salt* |
| ½ *cup sugar* | 1 *teaspoon cinnamon* |
| ½ *cup firmly packed light* | ½ *teaspoon cloves* |
|   *brown sugar* | ½ *teaspoon allspice* |
| 2 *eggs* | ¼ *teaspoon nutmeg* |
| 2 *cups sifted cake flour* | 1 *cup beer* |
| 2 *teaspoons baking powder* | |

Preheat oven to 350°. Grease an 8-inch-square pan.

Cream shortening. Gradually add sugar and blend well. Add eggs and beat.

Sift together all dry ingredients. Alternately add dry ingredients and beer to creamed mixture. Mix thoroughly. Pour batter into greased pan and bake 40 to 45 minutes.

## WORLD'S FAIR BELGIAN PAVILION BEER WAFFLES

3 *cups light beer*
3½ *cups flour*
½ *cup salad oil*
2 *eggs*
2 *tablespoons grated lemon rind*

1 *tablespoon vanilla*
1 *teaspoon lemon juice*
⅛ *teaspoon salt*
½ *pint heavy cream*
2 *tablespoons light brown sugar*

Combine all ingredients in a large mixing bowl. Beat mixture until smooth. Allow batter to stand 2 hours, or place in refrigerator overnight.

Spread batter very thinly on a hot, buttered waffle iron and bake waffles until lacy and crisp.

Serve waffles with whipped cream and a sprinkle of light brown sugar.

*Serves 6.*

## BROILED FROSTING

½ *cup margarine*
1 *cup firmly packed brown sugar*
1 *teaspoon vanilla*

*Approximately 2 tablespoons cream*
½ *cup chopped nuts*

Melt margarine and add brown sugar. Add vanilla and thin to spreading consistency with cream. Spread on cake, sprinkle with nuts, and place under broiler until it bubbles.

## CHOCOLATE BEER ICING

3 *tablespoons margarine*          2 *squares unsweetened*
2 *cups sifted confectioners'*         *chocolate*
   *sugar*                          2–3 *tablespoons beer*

Cream margarine and gradually add sugar. Beat well.

Melt chocolate; add to creamed mixture and stir well.

Stir in beer and beat until smooth and consistency is proper for spreading.

# Beverages
# and Sauces

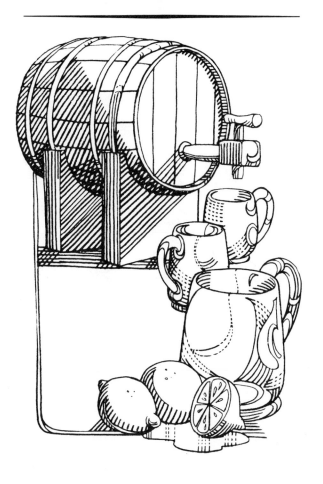

$A$lthough this chapter is thin, it is to be regarded as "the good thing that comes in the small package." We highly recommend the beverages as cool and refreshing and unusually tasty. There are many other beverages using beer as an ingredient, but these are the two we like best. In keeping with our feeling that everything great need not be time-consuming, we selected Barbie Shoolman's Barbecue Sauce as the all-time winner. It's imaginative, interesting, tasty, and fast. It leaves lots of time to sip those light and delectable Shandygaffs.

## SHANDYGAFF

1 *12-ounce can beer, chilled*    1 *7-ounce bottle ginger ale,*
*chilled*

Chill 2 12-ounce beer glasses in refrigerator. Pour half of 1 can beer and half of 1 bottle ginger ale into glass simultaneously, to ensure a large head.

*Serves 2.*

## LAGER LIME

2 *tablespoons lime juice*        1 *12-ounce can lager beer,*
    *(fresh or reconstituted)*        *chilled*

Chill 1 12- to 16-ounce beer glass. Pour in lime juice; pour in beer.

*Serves 1.*

## SAUCE MORNAY

Elegant and easy, this sauce is sure to enhance your vegetable dishes or favorite omelet.

1 *10¾-ounce can Cheddar*        2 *tablespoons margarine*
    *cheese soup*                2 *egg yolks, slightly beaten*
½ *cup beer*                    *Dash hot pepper sauce*
¼ *cup grated Parmesan*
    *cheese*

Blend soup, beer, cheese, and margarine in top of a double boiler. Cook 2 to 3 minutes, stirring occasionally until sauce is hot. Add egg yolks, stirring constantly. Add hot pepper sauce and cook 5 minutes longer, or until sauce thickens.

*Makes 2½ cups sauce.*

## BARBIE SHOOLMAN'S BARBECUE SAUCE

This perfectly marvelous concoction is not only easy to make, it requires no cooking, can be stored for several weeks in the refrigerator, or frozen for those culinary emergencies. We suggest marinating chicken or spareribs in this mixture, and it's delicious over any roasted meats, especially pork. Do try it!

2 14-ounce bottles catsup
1 12-ounce bottle chili sauce
⅓ cup prepared mustard
1 tablespoon dry mustard
1½ cups firmly packed
   brown sugar
1½ cups wine vinegar
1 cup fresh lemon juice

2 tablespoons ground
   pepper
½ cup A-1 Sauce
¼ cup Worcestershire sauce
1 tablespoon soy sauce
2 tablespoons salad oil
1 12-ounce can beer

Combine all ingredients and mix well.

*Makes over 2 quarts sauce.*

# Index

# Index

# Index